WILLIAMSF1

BIOGRAPHY

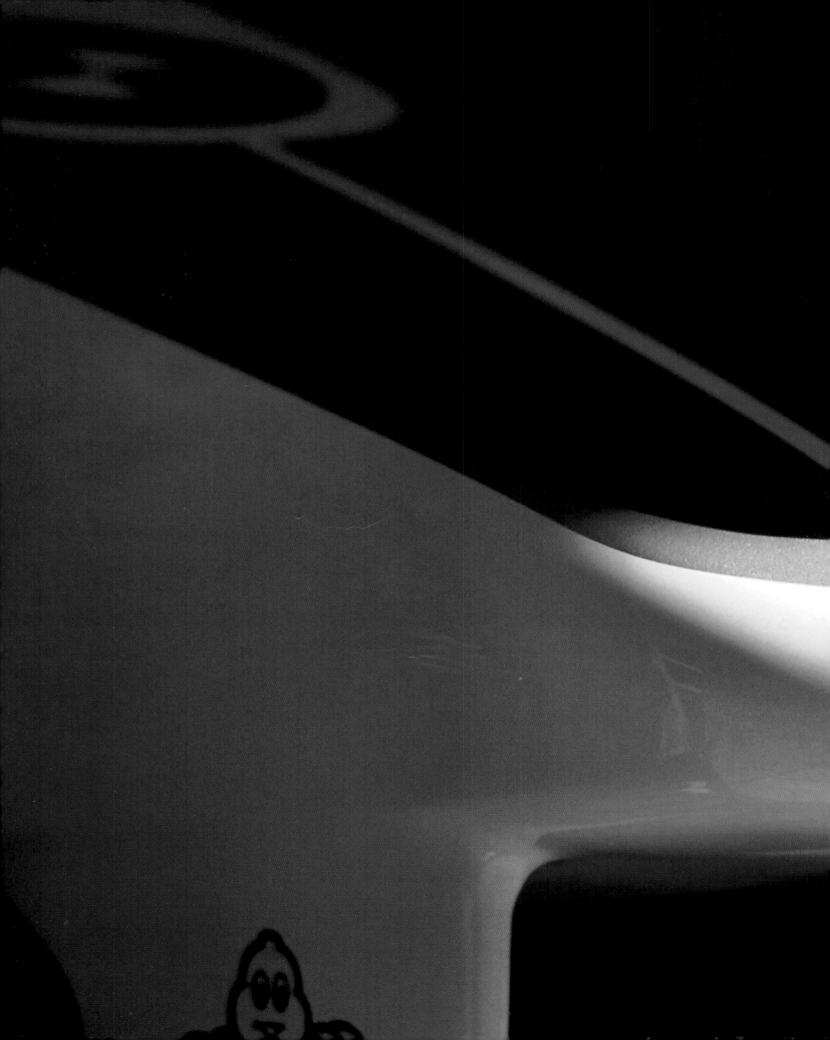

WILLIAMSF1
THE AUTHORISED PHOTOGRAPHIC
BIOGRAPHY

TEXT
ALAN HENRY

FOREWORD BY
FRANK WILLIAMS

ORION

Contents

Foreword by Frank Williams 6

1977-83

Sweet Taste of First Victory 8

The establishment of Williams Grand Prix Engineering in 1977 and the partnership with Australian driver Alan Jones... Keke Rosberg's 1982 title...Profile on Alan Jones

1984-88

Into the Championship Big Time 44

Williams and Honda at the cutting edge of a period of huge technological and commercial growth in F1...two Constructors' World Championships plus a Drivers' title for Nelson Piquet in 1987 ...Nigel Mansell establishes himself as a world class driver with the Williams F1 squad...Profile on Patrick Head

A New Partnership with Renault 80

Renault...Thierry Boutsen...Riccardo Patrese...
the celebrated returnee Nigel Mansell

Four Championships in Six Seasons 102

The golden years in Williams F1 history...Nigel Mansell (1992)...
Alain Prost (1993)...Damon Hill (1996)...
Jacques Villeneuve (1997)...the memorable, tragically short-lived
partnership with the great Ayrton Senna (1994)...
Profiles on Frank Williams and the team behind the scenes

Winners Again 168

A vibrant new partnership with BMW...the emergence
of Jenson Button, Ralf Schumacher and Juan Pablo Montoya...
Profile on Juan Pablo Montoya

WILLIAMSF1: Twenty-Five years at a Glance 214

Foreword

It is fair to say that I never expected, nor intended, to be where I am today. My interest in motor racing has been a lifelong fascination, but the path my involvement with the sport has steered me along could not possibly have been ordained. Every waking day I reflect that it has been an extraordinary privilege to be so intimately involved in one of the sporting world's most challenging and competitive activities.

Since my first forays into motor racing, WilliamsF1 has experienced its fair share of the highs and lows that a fortnightly contest on the world stage brings. And the highlights? It is quite simple really. Every single race win is reward enough and doubly so when we have managed to piece these wins into championship victories. But if there is a measure of what we have achieved, it is to compare the very humble origins of our embryonic organisation with the size and scale of WilliamsF1 today.

Despite the company physically changing beyond recognition over a quarter of a century, I believe we have managed to achieve something extraordinary in retaining a clear sense of our founding principles. The company as a whole today demonstrates a passion for racing, just as it did all those years ago when the first group of seventeen staff worked together to design and race the FW06.

Two of the most significant elements in the continued success of WilliamsF1 are undoubtedly an enduring partnership with Patrick Head and the loyalty and dedication of a very talented workforce. It is a measure of the organisation which we have all had a hand in building that a significant number of the first employees are still with us today, having made WilliamsF1 their lifelong career.

Pictures are intensely expressive, and there is no better way to illustrate the achievements and personalities with whom I have had the good fortune to participate throughout twenty-five very full years of Formula One.

FRANK WILLIAMS

CHAPTER ONE

Sweet Taste of First Victory

The 1977 season was a new beginning for Frank Williams. Having spent much of the previous decade struggling to survive in the hectic maelstrom that is Formula One, he went back to basics and started with a clean sheet.

Williams Grand Prix Engineering, the forerunner of WilliamsF1, was established on modest foundations. When one views the sleek, well-developed, high-technology image of Formula One racing in the first decade of the twenty-first century it is difficult to comprehend just how comparatively basic things were in the late 1970s. In those days only Ferrari built its car from the ground up. Everybody else purchased off-the-peg V8 engines from Cosworth Engineering in Northampton, bolted them into the back of their cars and went off to compete.

Financially, F1 was a much more modest affair. When Mario Andretti, the Lotus team leader, negotiated a deal to stay with the British team for £600,000 in 1978 this was considered an unimaginable sum of money to pay a driver. Many team budgets did not run anywhere near that astronomical figure. Running his Brabham-Ford for Piers Courage in 1969 had cost Frank between £40,000 and £50,000 for the season. Yet even by the time Frank and Patrick Head embarked on the 1978 season with the Williams FW06 driven by Alan Jones the costs had multiplied tenfold. The Cosworth engine that had cost £7500 a decade earlier now came with a price tag of £14,500, and the team used six of them, while a routine overhaul for one of these V8s cost £2500. However, by today's standards, this was bargain-basement stuff.

Moreover, back then, motor racing was a far more hazardous, wild and woolly affair than it has become today. Much work was progressing over safety developments, in terms of car construction and circuit design, but it was an unpredictable business, with the unwelcome possibility of injury ever present in people's minds.

But times were changing. The sport was evolving fast and its huge potential would soon be unlocked, with the Williams team poised to become one of its leading and most consistently successful players.

1977–83

Frank Williams out running with Alan Jones, the tough and ambitious Australian driver who signed with the team at the start of 1978. Signing Jones proved to be an astute and imaginative decision that paid off handsomely for both men. Frank was looking for a determined charger who would grow in status hand-in-hand with his team, while Jones, who'd scored a lucky win in the previous summer's Austrian Grand Prix at the wheel of an uncompetitive Shadow DN8,

was looking for a springboard to future success. Alan was thirty when he signed up with Williams and few shared his personal confidence that, one day, he would win a World Championship. He would prove all his critics wrong. Running was always an abiding passion in Frank's life until the road accident in 1986 that left him in a wheelchair. David Warren, a keen athlete who finished eighth in the 800 metres at the 1980 Moscow Olympics and later worked for Canon, one of the Williams team's sponsors, confirmed: 'I promise you, he was superbly fit. He would run six-minute miles and that's not jogging, by any means.'

BELOW Where it all began. By the start of the 1978 F1 season, Williams Grand Prix Engineering occupied an unremarkable factory adjacent to the railway line on the Station Road Industrial Estate in Didcot. Here Frank Williams and Patrick Head pose outside their premises together with the first of the Williams FW06s behind the team's transporter. This was the first bespoke, Patrick Head-designed Williams racing car designed and manufactured by the new company. In those days Grand Prix racing was a more haphazard and unpredictable affair than the professional, tightly focused and immaculately promoted TV spectacular that it has become in the first decade of the twenty-first century. Yet Frank's determination to succeed and establish his team as a credible front-line F1 force never wavered from the day this photograph was taken. For his part, Patrick was born into a world of motor racing and fast cars. His father, Colonel Michael Head, who had spent some time as a military adviser to the government's chief scientist, Sir Solly Zuckerman, was a keen amateur racer with various Jaguar sports cars during the 1950s. And that enthusiasm certainly rubbed off on his son.

RIGHT Alan Jones in the pits at Buenos Aires together with Patrick Head (right), prior to the start of the 1978 Argentine Grand Prix. Patrick would later admit that the experience of working with the Australian during the course of that year effectively shaped his attitude towards Formula One in the futur Prior to that, he frankly admitted that he'd regarded Grand Pri racing as a bit of fun, and in the back of his mind always had th thought that he might turn his hand to something completely different over the next few years. Working with Jones through 1978, on a racing car that he had almost completely designed from the ground up, took Patrick through what he regarded as a transitional phase in his professional life. Suddenly he bega to realise that the prospects for the Williams team were quite bright and, if everybody seriously got down to it, they might ev win a Grand Prix. And perhaps much more besides.

ABOVE In the late 1970s the first three rounds of the World Championship were held outside Europe, with the South African Grand Prix at Kyalami at the start of March following the Argentine and Brazilian races which usually took place during January. In both Buenos Aires and Rio de Janeiro Alan Jones was out of luck, but in South Africa he drove to a strong fourth place on the same lap as Ronnie Peterson's winning Lotus 78. It was clear from this performance that the Williams FW06 was an extremely promising Formula One car, but both Frank and Patrick knew that the team had to organise its infrastructure rather better over the coming months if consistent top-six results were going to be achieved.

LEFT Alan Jones signalled his true Formula One potential in the 1978 United States Grand Prix West, an event held in the sun-soaked streets of Long Beach, California, from 1976 to 1983. Having qualified the Williams FW06 on the fourth row of the starting grid, he quickly stormed through into third place and began closing in on the Ferraris driven by Gilles Villeneuve and Carlos Reutemann that were running first and second. Villeneuve then crashed out of the battle, leaving Jones to hold second place for more than twenty laps. Due to a manufacturing problem, the nose wing then collapsed to the point where its outer extremities were dragging on the circuit, as shown in this photograph. Amazingly, this hardly affected Jones's speed. It was only when a fuel pick-up problem developed over the final twenty laps that he dropped back through the pack to finish seventh. Yet one could hardly have placed a value on what Jones's performance had done to motivate the team. It was as if they could sniff impending success in the air.

RIGHT Alan Jones's run to second place in the 1978 United States Grand Prix East at Watkins Glen represented a triumph at the end of a troubled weekend for the team during which there seemed a fair chance that the Australian would not even be starting the race, much less finishing it strongly. During practice a front stub-axle broke as Jones was accelerating through a fast downhill right-hand corner at this beautiful circuit in upstate New York. Alan was very fortunate to escape without injury after the car ploughed into a trackside catch fence, but it was clear that he could not be permitted to drive the spare FW06 until Patrick had resolved the problems with the wheel hubs. In a characteristic display of F1 resourcefulness, Charlie Crichton-Stuart – an old friend of Frank's who had helped to secure Saudi Arabian sponsorship – persuaded a local engineering company in the nearby town of Elmira to open up specially and for its workforce to toil all night to heat-treat the remaining hubs. Jones then qualified third and finished second, having taken Patrick's word that all would be well.

Spirit of Formula One. Alan Jones's Williams FW06 speeds over the crest coming out of Monte Carlo's Casino Square during the 1978 Grand Prix through the streets of the Mediterranean principality. He ran strongly in this challenging event, but was eventually sidelined by an oil leak. Williams would win this race rarely over the years, and Jones was never victorious in Monaco, even though he drove superbly there in both 1980 and 1981 before mechanical misfortune intervened.

For the 1979 season, Patrick Head took a leaf out of Lotus founder Colin Chapman's book and developed the epochal Williams FW07. Patrick might regard it as something of an overstatement that the FW07 redrew the boundaries of contemporary F1 car performance. What it certainly did was propel technical thinking into a new era at a time when the intricacies and effects of the aerodynamic flow beneath the cars were proving to be hugely challenging for F1 engineers. In 1978, Chapman's Lotus 79 had been the class of the field. Alan Jones and the Williams FW07 developed into the most competitive partnership of the 1979 season and the new car carried Clay Regazzoni to the team's maiden F1 victory in the British Grand Prix at Silverstone. Yet, more crucially, designing this car convinced Patrick that Williams needed its own wind tunnel. In 2002 WilliamsF1's latest wind tunnel works in carefully structured shifts around the clock. In 1979 the entire aerodynamic design of the Williams FW07 was shaped by a week's work in the wind tunnel of London's Imperial College. It's a measure of how times have dramatically changed.

The team on the pit wall at Silverstone cheering on Regazzoni's victory in the 1979 British Grand Prix. It was ten years after Piers Courage had driven Frank's private Brabham BT26 to fifth place in the same race and the intervening years had seen Williams himself riding a wild roller coaster of raised hopes and sadly dashed ambitions. Now that elusive moment had finally arrived. On the right, wearing a Goodyear cap, is Ken Tyrrell, one of Frank's most respected rivals, who had made the characteristically generous gesture of leaving his own team's pit to celebrate the Williams success. Ten years earlier it had been Jackie Stewart who had won the British Grand Prix at the wheel of a Tyrrell-entered Matra-Ford. Now another of Ken's drivers, Jean-Pierre Jarier, would finish third behind Regazzoni and René Arnoux's Renault V6 turbo. Tyrrell admired Frank enormously, respecting his dedication and singlemindedness. It was certainly reciprocated: Frank retained huge regard for his rival British F1 team owner to the end of Tyrrell's life.

ABOVE That historic afternoon. The team members crowd the pit wall at Silverstone as Clay Regazzoni storms out of Woodcote Corner in the Williams FW07 to win the 1979 British Grand Prix at Silverstone. It was somewhat ironic that Regazzoni, the thirty-nine-year-old veteran who'd been taken on as the team's second driver at the start of the season, should be the one to score that emotional first victory for the team. Alan Jones had been quicker all year up to that point and, indeed, was running away with the race at Silverstone before his car came rolling into the pit lane trailing a haze of smoke and steam, the result of a cracked water pump. Team insiders recall Frank glancing at Jones's stricken car only for a second before refocusing his gaze on Regazzoni out on the circuit. It was bitterly disappointing for Jones, but he was history where that afternoon was concerned. Regazzoni was the man of the moment who could deliver on the day.

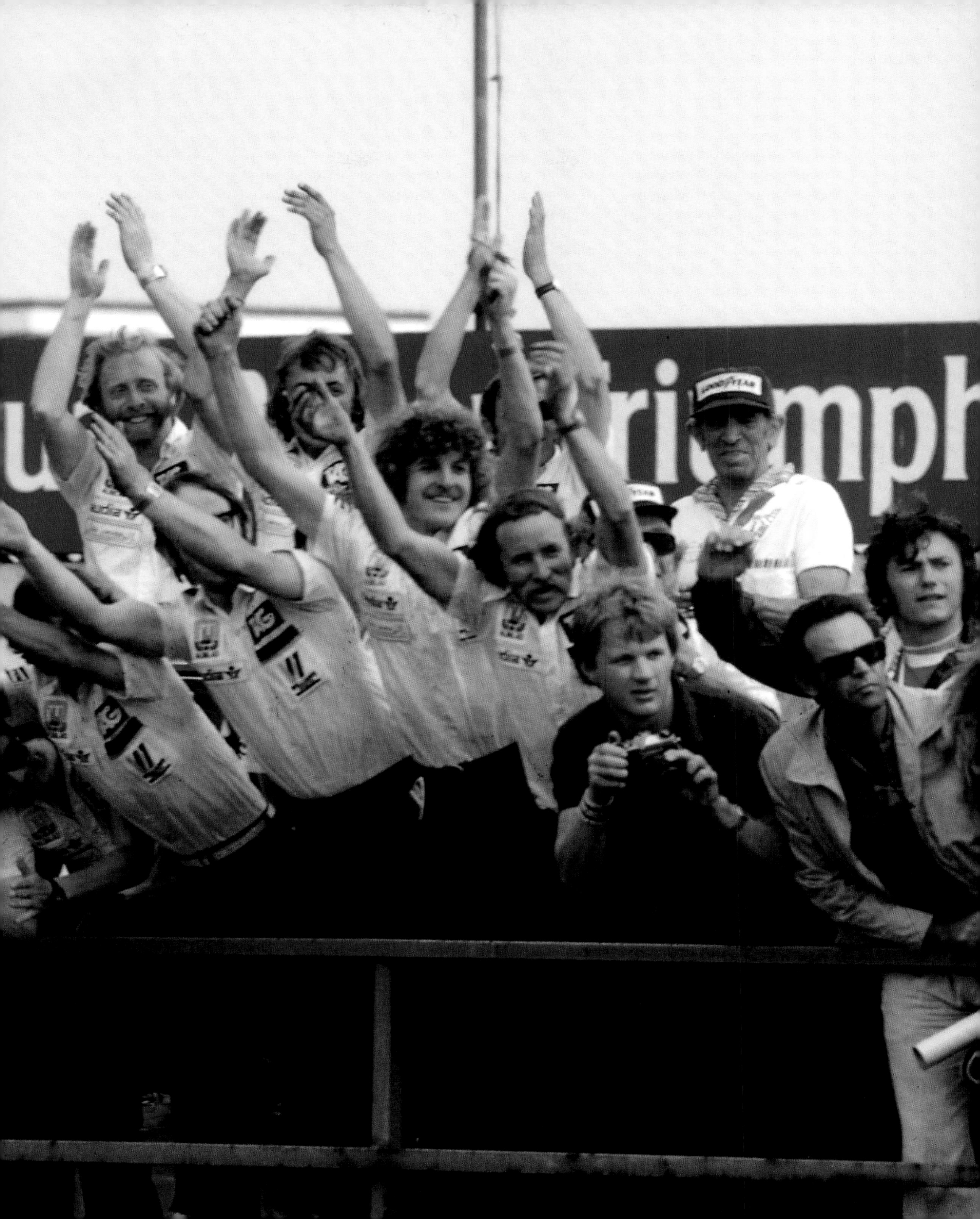
GOODYEAR

Jones and Regazzoni proved a strong partnership, with Alan following up Clay's victory in the 1979 British Grand Prix with impressive wins in the German, Austrian, Dutch and Canadian races. Yet there was never any question of offering one driver priority over the other in the Williams set-up. At Hockenheim, a fortnight after Clay's success at Silverstone, Jones was slowing towards the end of the race with a slow puncture in a rear tyre. He had dominated the Grand Prix, but now he was being forced to ease his pace. Some teams might well have signalled their second driver to slow down in order to preserve the leader's advantage. But this is rarely the case at Williams. Both Frank and Patrick believe that the racing drivers they employ are highly qualified professionals who can keep out of trouble, particularly with each other. On that afternoon, Jones just scraped home to win by 2.9 seconds. It was the first one–two finish to be achieved by the team.

Regazzoni sweeps round Stowe Corner on his way to victory at Silverstone. When Williams expanded its team to run a second car for 1979, many F1 insiders expected Frank to gamble and take a chance on a newcomer. Instead, they opted for the mustachioed Swiss driver who already had a decade of F1 racing behind him. The rationale behind this decision was as considered as it was logical. Frank and Patrick felt it was better to opt for a man experienced and seasoned in the ways of F1 rather than a wide-eyed novice. Their priority was to build and expand the team steadily and in a structured, measured fashion. Just as he had been at Ferrari between 1970 and 1976, Clay proved a fine team player. Fast, consistent and reliable, he was very much the right man at the right time for Williams. Poignantly, he had made his F1 debut for Ferrari in the 1970 Dutch Grand Prix at Zandvoort. It was the race that claimed the life of Piers Courage at the wheel of Frank's de Tomaso.

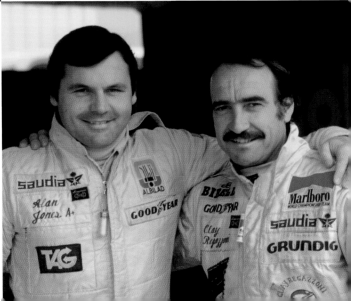

The start of the 1979 Dutch Grand Prix at Zandvoort with Alan Jones just edging
his Williams FW07 into the lead ahead of Gilles Villeneuve's Ferrari 312T4,
Didier Pironi's Tyrrell, Mario Andretti's Lotus and the other Williams FW07,
driven by Clay Regazzoni. Take a close look at Clay's car. That's right: its left front
wheel is missing, torn off moments earlier in a brush with René Arnoux's Renault.
Clay would three-wheel round the first corner and pull to a halt on the grass,
his race well and truly run. That would leave Jones to battle memorably with
Villeneuve for the lead, eventually taking a commanding win after his rival
spun off with a puncture and then wrecked the rear of his Ferrari by trying
to drive it back to the pits on three tyres and a wheel rim. Alan would
eventually finish ahead of Villeneuve's team-mate Jody Scheckter and
Ligier driver Jacques Laffite. The seaside circuit near Haarlem was always
a great favourite with the F1 fraternity and everybody was sorry when
the last Grand Prix took place there in 1985.

profile

Alan Jones

Alan Jones and the Williams team came together at a time when nobody else in the F1 pit lane was much interested in either of them. By the end of 1977 Jones had a single, lucky victory under his belt, achieved in that year's Austrian Grand Prix at the wheel of a Shadow DN8. Williams had not much more than a private March 761, a small factory base and a youthful Patrick Head sketching the preliminary drawings for his first genuine F1 car, the FW06.

'Williams and I came together at just the right time,' recalled Jones. 'Frank was always very competitive, but at the same time I never saw him be impolite. He was very controlled, but also determined and intelligent. Even when we had the odd argument or confrontation, it was a question of being bollocked and then it was over and on to the next item.'

By the start of the 1979 season Jones seemed to have broken through the crucial barrier of self-belief that confronts every professional racing driver at some time in his career. He epitomised Frank's and Patrick's feelings about what an F1 driver should be and how he should behave. In that respect, many of the subsequent Williams F1 drivers had difficulty matching up to his template.

Jones didn't need an emotional life-support system when he was out of the cockpit. A sympathetic arm around the shoulder would not have been welcomed in moments of stress or disappointment. This hard-driving Australian was very much a man's man and operating in a man's world. He was also a great yardstick for the team's development. As the first winning Williams – the FW07 – came on stream in 1979, everybody in the team knew full well that Alan was giving 100 per cent. His technical debriefs might have been succinct and to-the-point and his dry humour would often be deployed to push the responsibility for a disappointing performance on to the designer's shoulders, but he motivated the team in a towering fashion. He had the air of a man whose time had come and who was with the right collaborators at the right moment. In particular, Jones had huge faith in Patrick Head's ability to engineer and manufacture a solid, competitive and thoroughly secure racing car.

'I always knew that when Patrick designed a new car he designed one that was both very quick and as safe as he could make it. One of the best things about staying with a team for a long time is that you can build up faith in the organisation. And I certainly did that during my time with Williams.'

RIGHT Alan Jones drove a great race at the daunting Osterreichring circuit to win the 1979 Austrian Grand Prix despite grappling with gear-change trouble which slowed his Williams FW07 in the closing stages of the race. Here Frank and the team celebrate his success with delight from the pit wall. It was Jones's second straight win after Hockenheim and the team's third in a row since Regazzoni won the British Grand Prix. Suddenly that summer Williams had clicked. Not only did the team have a great car, but it was also learning much about the subtleties of operating a team in the F1 front line. Yet there was never any overt elation about this performance breakthrough, simply a quiet and measured satisfaction. Frank, for one, was sufficiently seasoned in the capricious ways of the F1 business not to get too comfortable with success, or indeed take anything for granted.

LEFT Jones became embroiled in one of the best races of the 1979 World Championship season when he found himself pitched into a dramatic wheel-to-wheel confrontation with Gilles Villeneuve's Ferrari during the Canadian Grand Prix at Montreal. Villeneuve had led the opening stages only for Jones to summon up all his reserves of courage and commitment to forge past under braking for the tight hairpin just before the pits. Thereafter Alan strained every sinew to open a fractional lead over the determined French Canadian ace: 'but if I relaxed long enough simply to take a deep breath, that scarlet shitbox was filling my mirrors again'. Jones eventually won the 72-lap, 197-mile race by just over a second from Villeneuve, a man he admired enormously and rightly regarded as one of his most formidable rivals throughout his F1 career.

LEFT As part of the process of growing to maturity, the team bade farewell to the popular Clay Regazzoni at the end of the 1979 season and replaced him with Argentine driver Carlos Reutemann. Moody, inconsistent, but brilliant on his day and regarded by many as the one driver apart from Stirling Moss who never won a World Championship while certainly deserving to do so, Reutemann's arrival meant that the team now had two cars able to run genuinely at the front of the pack. Here Carlos celebrates after winning the 1980 Monaco Grand Prix with his wife Mimicha (in sunglasses) beneath the approving gaze of Princess Grace and Prince Rainier. After a dismal 1979 season with Lotus, Reutemann was happy to sign as Jones's number two. 'When you are a starving man, you eat rabbit food, if necessary,' he said thoughtfully. 'You are thankful for anything you can get.'

RIGHT Alan Jones with Frank Williams early in the 1980 season. The rugged Australian had by this stage developed an aura of unstoppable self-confidence that was certainly aided by the superb performance of the Williams FW07. Those four race wins in 1979 had given him a taste of what he might now be able to achieve, and in 1980 would deliver on that promise in spectacular style. Both Frank and Patrick Head found him extremely easy to work with in the sense that he almost always gave his best. Yet he was never reticent if he reckoned a problem was not of his making. As he gained confidence and self-assurance, he would sometimes say directly to Patrick, 'I want you to know, Patrick, that *you* are in the shit,' when referring to some deficiency in the car's performance. He was fit and tough behind the wheel, but never in the slightest neurotic or obsessive about his job. Driving was driving for Alan Jones; it was as simple as that.

LEFT One of Jones's most memorable victories came in the 1980 French Grand Prix at Paul Ricard where a gamble to use bigger-diameter front tyres than the rival Ligiers saw the Australian driver's Williams FW07 decisively trounce his Gallic rivals. This win came at an emotional time for the whole F1 fraternity as political developments behind the scenes polarised the British and French competitors. The French were all believed to be aligned with the sport's governing body, the FIA, while the British teams lined up behind the Formula One Constructors' Association as these two organisations battled for control of the sport's commercial rights and lucrative television income. Frank's patriotic enthusiasm was certainly stirred by this victory, especially when Jones took his place atop the rostrum above Didier Pironi and Jacques Laffite, whose Ligiers had finished second and third.

Marlboro
British Grand Prix

The 1980 British Grand Prix at Brands Hatch saw Jones score another commanding victory on the first anniversary of the team's first F1 win at Silverstone. Brands Hatch was a very different track and the high levels of downforce generated by the latest breed of ground-effect car left onlookers staggered at the lap speeds produced. The Brands Hatch success came in the middle of a season in which Jones had already won in Argentina and France and would go on to post victories in Canada and the USA to set the seal on his World Championship title. He is seen on the winner's rostrum celebrating with Nelson Piquet, whose Brabham had finished second.

Carlos Reutemann on his way to second place behind Nelson Piquet's Brabham in the 1980 German Grand Prix at Hockenheim. The Argentinian driver admitted he had to recalibrate his approach to driving in order to handle such a competitive car. By his own admission, that was no easy task. The previous year's Lotus 79 had not been on the pace and now Reutemann found it took some time to get the best out of the car's extraordinary adhesion. By the end of the season, however, Reutemann's driving rehabilitation would be complete and he would be ready to challenge Jones for the 1981 World Championship.

A Saudia sponsor and Williams team member Ian Anderson (right) celebrate on the track at Montreal, as Jones storms home to win the 1980 Canadian Grand Prix and put the year's World Championship crown beyond doubt. This had been a distinctly fraught race as title rivals Jones and Nelson Piquet had collided at the first corner, triggering a multiple pile-up that had resulted in the Grand Prix being stopped and restarted. Piquet had to use his spare Brabham and, at the restart, hurtled away to build up a substantial lead before his engine failed spectacularly. Thereafter Jones had it all under control and led to the finish ahead of his team-mate Carlos Reutemann. It was the team's third one–two of the season. Their next one-two, at the start of the following season, would cause more aggravation than delight.

Jones rounded off the 1980 season by clinching the championship at Montreal. Here he is interviewed on the winner's rostrum by Jackie Stewart. Shortly after this success, Jones returned to his homeland in order to take part in the non-championship Australian Grand Prix, a race that meant a great deal to him as it had been won by his late father Stan more than two decades before. Jones duly won the race and privately admitted that it was as important to him as most rounds of the official title chase. It was certainly a symbolic homecoming.

RIGHT Alan Jones's Saudia Williams FW07B won the opening race of the 1981 season proper through the streets of Long Beach on the third anniversary of that memorable showing in the agile little Williams FW06. Reutemann had led early on, but was baulked by a slower car with the result that the rugged Jones saw a gap and shot past the Argentinian driver to take over at the front of the pack. This hardly delighted Carlos who eased back to finish a distant runner-up over twenty seconds behind Jones. Tensions were already building up between these two highly motivated drivers who, although comparable in terms of speed and commitment, had very different personalities. Frank has subsequently admitted that he took a very masculine attitude towards his drivers, feeling that they should all radiate Jones's self-contained, devil-may-care approach. But, on reflection, he believes the team would have eked even more out of Reutemann had they showed their appreciation of his talents more openly.

ABOVE The lid finally came off the simmering rivalry between the two Williams drivers in explosive fashion after the 1981 Brazilian Grand Prix at Rio de Janeiro. Here Reutemann is seen leading Jones during this rain-soaked event which the Argentinian driver won against team orders, prompting a furious response from Jones who was just riding along a few seconds behind him, believing that Carlos would abide by the terms of his contract. The deal was that if Jones was less than seven seconds behind, Reutemann would have to let the Australian overtake. On this occasion he didn't. Jones was furious and let his team know precisely what he felt behind the closed garage doors in the paddock at the end of the race. From now on, the two men would hardly speak to each other, although they were clever enough to know that they had mutually advantageous technical contributions to make to the overall team effort.

LEFT The victory podium at Rio de Janeiro following the 1981 Brazilian Grand Prix with an empty place to the left of winner Reutemann and third-place finisher Riccardo Patrese. Alan Jones flatly refused to join Carlos after that controversial race, in which he believed he was double-crossed by his colleague. Williams told Reutemann that he had broken his contract and he was not paid anything for the win. Reutemann never mentioned the question of his prize money, an illustration of just what an intelligent operator he was. He cleverly avoided an argument that he was not going to win.

Carlos Reutemann on his way to a disappointing tenth place in the 1981 French Grand Prix at Dijon-Prenois. This season saw the Formula One business racked by a continuation of the rivalry between the major car makers – represented by Renault and Ferrari – and the smaller specialist teams that made up the remainder of the field and of which Williams was one of the most competitive. One by-product of the tension produced by this situation had been the withdrawal of tyre suppliers Goodyear at the start of the season, leaving the French Michelin brand servicing the whole field. When Goodyear returned to F1 midway through the year it was to supply just Williams and its key British rival, the Bernie Ecclestone-owned Brabham team. The French race marked the occasion of their return.

Williams chief mechanic Allan Challis puts the finishing touches to Jones's FW07B during practice for the 1981 British Grand Prix at Silverstone. Competing in their home round of the World Championship would always suffuse the patriotic Williams squad with a particular buzz of excitement, especially as the race had a strong sentimental place in their minds since Clay Regazzoni's memorable victory in 1979. Jones would be as competitive as ever in 1981, but was eliminated in a multiple collision at the end of the opening lap when he was taken off by Gilles Villeneuve's out-of-control Ferrari turbo. Reutemann ultimately finished second to John Watson's McLaren-Ford.

Just prior to the 1981 Italian Grand Prix Alan Jones became involved in an incident that highlighted just what a freewheeling and independent soul he was. Having been embroiled in a territorial dispute over the same piece of London's Chiswick High Road with the occupants of a Transit van, Jones arrived at Monza with a broken finger on his right hand as a consequence of the physical fracas that had ensued. As a result, Jones's right hand was heavily bandaged throughout the race weekend. Frank Williams was extremely cross with Jones, but not because of this brawl. Alan told Frank he was retiring from racing at the end of the year and his employer retorted that he was 'bloody inconsiderate' leaving it so late in the day to make such an announcement.

Alan Jones started the 1981 German Grand Prix at Hockenheim battling wheel-to-wheel with Alain Prost's Renault turbo for the lead of the race, but finished it in a dejected tenth place after a repeat of the fuel-feed problems that had lost him the lead at Monaco a few weeks earlier. Without these unfortunate technical problems Jones would have almost certainly won both races and been in a strong position to challenge for a second consecutive World Championship. Jones took these setbacks in his philosophical stride: the team had now assumed the role of seasoned front runner so there was absolutely no point in telling any of its members that they had let their driver down. They were too professional and focused for that.

RIGHT Carlos Reutemann was leading the World Championship by a single point going into the somewhat bizarre Caesars Palace Grand Prix in Las Vegas. The circuit was laid out in the massive public car parks of the legendary gaming hotel. Carlos blitzed the opposition to take pole position, then unaccountably faded in the race, finishing seventh and losing the title to Nelson Piquet by one point. By his own admission, Carlos's usual capacity to retain every detail of his car's technical set-up and precise chassis adjustments deserted him on that day. In the Saturday free practice he collided lightly with Piquet's Brabham and his Williams FW07B never handled properly again. In the race he complained of a problem with the gear-change and never challenged. Jones won the Grand Prix commandingly on his last outing for Williams. Here he celebrates (BELOW), on the winner's rostrum at Las Vegas, a dominant victory ahead of Alain Prost,

who finished second, and the newly crowned World Champion Nelson Piquet. By this stage a disappointed Reutemann had slunk away to reflect on a title lost. He and Jones would never meet again and Reutemann's career with the team would end with his abrupt retirement after only two races in 1982. Yet the Argentinian driver would remain a close friend of Frank Williams. Early in 1990, when Aerolineas

Argentinas reopened its Buenos Aires to London service for the first time since the Falklands War eight years earlier, Reutemann was one of the celebrity guests on the inaugural flight. On his arrival he took a taxi to Paddington and then a train to Didcot. He phoned Frank from a callbox at the station: he'd come to visit his old friend and employer.

ABOVE Frank Williams and Patrick Head pulled out all the stops in a bid to persuade Alan Jones to reverse his decision to retire at the end of 1981. After his victory in the Caesars Palace Grand Prix, the Williams directors persuaded the Australian driver to come to the UK for a secret test in the revolutionary Williams six-wheeler, the FW07B, that they were considering using for 1982. With its four tiny rear wheels, all of which were driven, the six-wheeler certainly left Jones pretty impressed. But it was not enough to persuade him to change his mind and return to Formula One.

BELOW The rear end of the 1982 Williams FW08B six-wheeler reflected some ingenious technical thinking on the part of Patrick Head and his engineers. Williams were still using Cosworth engines, and these traditional 3-litre V8s were becoming somewhat breathless in terms of performance against the emerging breed of 1.5-litre turbocharged engines. Consequently there was a premium on picking up every tenth of a second that might be available. After completing some detailed calculations, Patrick concluded that the large conventional rear tyres used were responsible for around 40 per cent of the aerodynamic drag generated by the car. His wind-tunnel calculations pointed to the conclusion that a six-wheeler, using four small rear wheels to do the driving, would offer a significant performance improvement. Despite further evaluation tests the project never raced and the FIA specifically banned six-wheelers at the start of 1983.

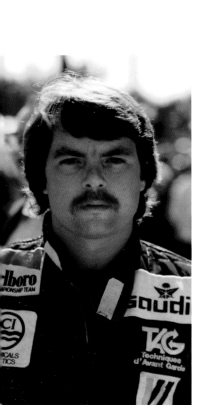

Keke Rosberg joined the Williams team at the start of the 1982 season.
The chain-smoking Finn used to joke irreverently about Frank and Patrick
that 'they've never quite forgiven me for not being Alan Jones'. It was easy to
see what he meant. The team's thinking on the subject of drivers had largely
been shaped by Jones and he'd been the man leading the team through that
transitional phase from wide-eyed also-ran to established winner. Now there
had to be a period of readjustment. Frank approached both Niki Lauda and
John Watson, but neither was available. Rosberg, who'd driven for the
Fittipaldi team the previous year, proved quick from the moment he first
tested a Williams at Paul Ricard. He had an extrovert, almost swashbuckling
style that didn't always sit easily with Patrick's pragmatic and analytical
approach. Yet they rubbed along well during 1982 and gradually worked out
a good professional relationship . . . And Keke won the World Championship.

LEFT After Carlos Reutemann retired following the 1982 Brazilian Grand Prix, Frank Williams spent some time considering precisely who would be the most suitable candidate to partner Rosberg for the balance of the season. As a temporary expedient they signed the forty-two-year-old former World Champion Mario Andretti to have a one-off outing in the other FW07C in the US Grand Prix West at Long Beach. Unfortunately the veteran American driver glanced off a wall early in the race and was forced to retire. It was a disappointing day for the popular Andretti who had won this same race five years earlier at the wheel of a Lotus 78 after a great battle with Jody Scheckter's Wolf and Niki Lauda's Ferrari.

ABOVE Keke Rosberg really demonstrated his potential with a strong drive to second place in the 1982 US Grand Prix West at Long Beach behind Niki Lauda's McLaren. The street circuit through the Californian coastal city was quicker than Monaco, but imposed the same disciplines of meticulous judgement and restraint on the competing drivers. The Finn never put a wheel wrong throughout this particular race, demonstrating that he had the makings of a well-rounded and complete F1 talent. Rosberg says that he absolutely loved his time as a Williams driver: 'I had a tremendous time there and will always be very grateful for the break they gave me,' he said more than a decade later. 'They were a very special bunch of people.'

LEFT As Rosberg's full-time team-mate for the 1982 season Frank Williams finally opted for the pleasant Irish driver Derek Daly. Williams would later confess that he had sometimes been a little too conservative in his driver selection, and would admit subsequently that 'we should have been braver'. But, in fairness to Daly, it was difficult to see what better option was available two races into the season once Reutemann had made his surprise decision to retire. At the end of the season Daly, who was close to Rosberg's race pace but could never match him in qualifying, was replaced in the Williams line-up by Jacques Laffite.

RIGHT The 1982 Monaco Grand Prix proved to be a remarkable race of changing fortunes which Derek Daly might have won in the Williams FW08 had he not spun and knocked off his car's rear wing in the closing stages. Yet Daly's was only the last in a succession of misfortunes that afflicted three potential winners in addition to himself. Alain Prost's Renault spun into a barrier as a light rain shower doused the circuit with just over two laps to go; then Riccardo Patrese's Brabham took the lead, only to spin at the Loews Hairpin; then Didier Pironi's Ferrari turbo briefly led before running out of fuel in the tunnel. So Daly suddenly found himself fleetingly in the lead, but his disastrous pirouette had also smashed the FW08's gearbox casing and removed its oil pump. The Irishman ground to a halt and gained scant consolation to be classified a distant sixth as the recovering Patrese retook the lead to win.

Keke Rosberg in the Williams-Cosworth FW08 which carried him most of the way to his World Championship title in 1982. After relying on evolutionary versions of the epochal FW07 design since 1979, Williams introduced a totally new car for 1982 that put into practice many technical lessons learned with the earlier car. Most notably, in the interests of lighter weight and aerodynamic efficiency, the front suspension was completely redesigned, doing away with the bulky fabricated rocker arms that activated the spring/dampers and replacing them with a tidier and more compact pullrod configuration. The team debuted the FW08 in the 1982 Belgian Grand Prix at Zolder, after using the uprated FW07C in the long-haul races outside Europe. Rosberg almost won on the new car's maiden outing, but locked its rear brakes while leading a couple of laps from the finish, handing victory to John Watson's McLaren.

BELOW AND RIGHT Rosberg won just a single race during his successful quest for the 1982 World Championship in a year when no individual driver managed more than two victories. Yet as this shot dramatically shows, he came within half a length of victory in the Austrian Grand Prix at the Osterreichring, denied by Elio de Angelis in the distinctive black-and-gold Lotus-Ford. Keke's sole victory – over Prost's Renault turbo – would come in the Swiss Grand Prix at the Dijon-Prenois circuit in central France. This apparent geographical anomaly reflected the fact that circuit racing had been banned in Switzerland since 1955 and borrowing the Swiss epithet enabled a second round of the World Championship to be held within France in a single year.

RIGHT Rosberg with the legendary television commentator Murray Walker after celebrating his victory in the 1982 Swiss Grand Prix at Dijon-Prenois. Alain Prost looked set for a commanding victory, but his Renault turbo slowed in the closing stages with a damaged aerodynamic side-skirt that badly compromised the car's handling over the last few laps of the race. Rosberg was closing in relentlessly on the crippled French machine when Peter Collins, the Williams team manager, noticed an official on the startline moving to unfurl the chequered flag. Suspecting that the partisan official might be about to flag the race to its finish while the French car was still ahead, Collins rushed to the rostrum and managed to distract the fellow concerned. The race ran its full eighty-lap distance and Keke got through to take the lead when Prost ran wide on the penultimate lap.

Diana Ross (far left) might have been the most famous celebrity on the winner's rostrum after the 1982 Caesars Palace Grand Prix at Las Vegas, but even the singing star seemed rather swept aside in the jubilation surrounding Rosberg's World Championship clincher. Keke is seen here on the rostrum after his fifth-place finish in this final race of the season guaranteed him the title crown by five points from Didier Pironi and John Watson, who dead-heated for second place in the standings. Watson is also on the rostrum after finishing second in this race behind the Tyrrell of first-time F1 winner Michele Alboreto. After telephoning his parents to tell them of his life's ambition realised, Rosberg relaxed with a cigarette and a large slice of chocolate cake. He never really was a health-food fanatic.

One of the most far-sighted decisions taken by the Williams team in 1983 was to offer a test drive to the young Brazilian Ayrton Senna, who would go on to win that year's British Formula 3 Championship. Senna was instantly quick in the revised Williams FW08C when he tried it at Donington Park, matching the team's regular test driver Jonathan Palmer. But another decade would pass before Frank would get Ayrton's signature on a Williams F1 contract. The 1983 season proved to be a year of transition for the team, which started its World Championship assault with the FW08C, a reworked version of the car in which Keke Rosberg had won the World Championship. It had much shorter side-pods and a flat underside to conform with the new F1 technical regulations designed to reduce the amount of aerodynamic downforce generated by the inverted wing-section side-pods used at the height of the ground-effect generation.

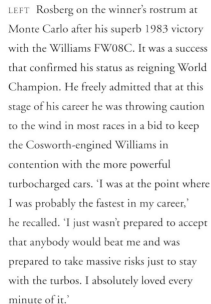

LEFT Rosberg on the winner's rostrum at Monte Carlo after his superb 1983 victory with the Williams FW08C. It was a success that confirmed his status as reigning World Champion. He freely admitted that at this stage of his career he was throwing caution to the wind in most races in a bid to keep the Cosworth-engined Williams in contention with the more powerful turbocharged cars. 'I was at the point where I was probably the fastest in my career,' he recalled. 'I just wasn't prepared to accept that anybody would beat me and was prepared to take massive risks just to stay with the turbos. I absolutely loved every minute of it.'

ABOVE LEFT One might have been forgiven for thinking that Rosberg was slightly overweight, although at fractionally over ten stones during his World Championship heyday he clearly was not. Keke would stay with Williams for a total of four years between 1982 and 1985, steadily developing his overall ability as a Grand Prix driver during that time. Frank Williams recalled that Keke really began to flourish as he did more testing and accumulated more experience at the wheel of a competitive F1 car. Williams sometimes wondered whether he perhaps short-changed himself by not spending sufficient time in the team's technical debriefs because he unquestionably showed himself to be extremely intelligent. In particular, he always impressed the team with his judgement when it came to tyre choice. He almost always selected the most suitable compound for a given situation, apparently by feel.

LEFT Keke Rosberg's victory in the 1983 Monaco Grand Prix was probably the best of his career. The team gambled to begin the race on dry-weather slick tyres even though the track had been doused by a rain shower shortly before the start. Keke pulled away in the early stages of this classic event and by the time the track dried out, most of his rivals were either too far behind or wrestling with the wrong tyres. At the time of this win, Williams were deep in negotiations with the Japanese Honda company for a contract to use their factory-prepared turbocharged engines on a long-term basis from the start of 1984. The rest of the Grand Prix field had opted for the more powerful turbocharged engine route and now it was time for Williams to follow suit, despite having invested considerable sums on a bespoke development programme to generate more power from the previously ubiquitous Cosworth V8 engine they had used exclusively up to that point.

ABOVE Jacques Laffite in the Williams-Cosworth FW08C on his way to fifth place in the 1983 San Marino Grand Prix at Imola. Frank Williams reduced his retainer for the 1984 season to reflect the Frenchman's disappointing form the previous year. It was typical of Jacques's good-humoured nature that he accepted this reduction in income without any undue bad feeling or complaint. The fact that Frank had Laffite under contract for 1984 meant he was unable to sign up Senna instead, a frustrating setback at a time when the tempo of F1 competition was intensifying.

CHAPTER TWO

Into the Championship Big Time

By the start of the 1984 season it was clear that the whole complexion of Formula One was changing dramatically. The emergence of turbocharged engine technology had strengthened the presence of major car manufacturers on the F1 scene and it had become increasingly clear that a partnership with such a manufacturer was a necessary prerequisite for future success. By the start of 1984 Williams had struck its deal with Honda; BMW was in partnership with Brabham; Ferrari's turbocharged engine programme had reached a sophisticated level of development; and McLaren had commissioned Porsche to make its bespoke turbo V6 that would carry Niki Lauda to his third World Championship by the end of that season.

In 1984 Keke Rosberg scored the first Williams-Honda F1 victory in Dallas, Texas. The following year the team introduced its first carbon-fibre composite chassis – the FW10 – which won four races, two each for Rosberg and the team's new signing, Nigel Mansell.

For 1986 Nelson Piquet was signed to drive alongside Mansell, but the year was mostly remembered for the road accident that left Frank Williams paralysed and facing the rest of his life as a paraplegic. With great determination, he was back at work before the end of the season and remained resolutely committed to furthering the aims and ambitions of his team, which duly clinched the Constructors' Championship that year.

The 1987 season saw Mansell and Piquet in their own private battle for the World Championship, with the Brazilian driver taking the third title of his career. At the end of the season Honda terminated its partnership with Williams and the team struggled through 1988 using Judd V8 engines, with Mansell and Riccardo Patrese as the driving team.

1984–88

Keke Rosberg in the Williams-Honda FW09B during the 1984 Dutch Grand Prix at Zandvoort where he ran in the top six for virtually the whole race before running out of fuel in the closing stages to be placed an eventual eighth. Keke had climbed as high as third place before the FW09B rolled silently into the Williams pit right under the nose of Nobuhiko Kawamoto, the Honda president. This disappointment came on the back of three broken engines in practice and made Honda appreciate that it needed to raise the standard of its game. Rosberg, for all his criticism of the way the FW09B handled, always credited Patrick Head with 'being almost entirely responsible' for educating Honda as to what was precisely required from a contemporary F1 engine. The biggest problem with this Williams was that it understeered – a characteristic by which the front end of the car wants to run wide, away from the apex of a corner – turning into a vicious oversteering slide as the Honda engine chimed in with all its power midway through the corner. It was quite a handful.

Keke Rosberg continued as Williams team leader throughout the 1984 season, his third with the team. The yellow ICI-branded overalls he wore that year were regarded at the time as terribly extrovert and offended the sensibilities of F1's traditionalists. Yet such a development was reflective of precisely what a commercially driven business F1 had become and the consequent need to maximise every ounce of promotional potential at a time when the investment necessary to sustain a competitive Grand Prix operation was steadily increasing. For all his skill behind the wheel of an F1 car, Rosberg continued to project a somewhat volatile and impulsive temperament when it came to dealing with Frank Williams and Patrick Head. During the summer of 1984, when the team was struggling to develop the new Honda V6 turbocharged engine in the Williams FW09B, Keke and Patrick exchanged some harsh words. Keke went to Frank and said, 'I'm leaving.' Frank said 'You're not.' Just as well. Had Keke accepted an offer from the flagging Renault F1 team for 1985 his career might have ended there and then.

Frank Williams confers with a Goodyear engineer in the pit lane at Detroit during the summer of 1984. In that season the team was definitely fighting against the prevailing tide. The rival Michelin-shod McLaren-TAGs of Alain Prost and Niki Lauda would win twelve out of the season's sixteen races while Williams, armed with the new FW09B powered by a Honda engine that was still very much in the early stages of its development, would post just a single victory in the one-off Dallas Grand Prix on a makeshift circuit in the Texan city. The team would use Goodyear tyres through to the company's withdrawal from F1 at the end of the 1997 season, then Bridgestones from 1998 to 2000, before forging a deal to race with Michelin rubber from the start of 2001. The complex technology of tyre development has always required a close collaboration between tyre maker and team, and Williams have been particularly aware and astute in this respect.

A 1984 post-practice debrief for the Williams team. Today you will find that every team has an army of engineers that disappears behind the tinted windows of a large motorhome in order to analyse every computer-monitored facet of their cars' performance in air-conditioned solace and comfort. Two decades ago things were very different and the paddock environment distinctly less formal. Here (from left to right), Frank Williams, team engineer Neil Oatley, Jacques Laffite, Patrick Head and Keke Rosberg sit in a group on garden chairs discussing the performance of the FW09Bs. There was precious little in the way of computerised assistance in those days; the cars' performance and every change to their set-ups were laboriously recorded by Frank on sheets in his own personal folder.

Keke Rosberg battles with Niki Lauda's McLaren-TAG for track position in the 1984 Dutch Grand Prix. In many ways Rosberg and Lauda – and the cars they were driving that year – were as different as chalk and cheese. Keke had built up a reputation for projecting an audacious, slightly wild and extrovert driving style, never seemingly happier than when he was sliding the tail of his car in a huge oversteering drift. Niki was the ascetic, analytical competitor who drove with an almost geometric precision, happy to develop his chassis set-up to the point where the car took as much of the strain out of the business of driving as was possible. The contrast between the Williams-Honda FW09B and the McLaren-TAG MP4/2 was similarly extreme. Williams was very much feeling its way while developing a version of an existing engine. The McLaren was powered by a bespoke, tailor-made V6 paid for by the team's investors and configured absolutely to the precise design requirements of technical director John Barnard, a friend and contemporary of Patrick Head.

The Honda RA163 V6 installed in the engine bay of the Williams-Honda FW09B, a photograph which emphasises just how complicated a business packaging an F1 engine into a chassis can be. The first Williams-Honda FW09s had made their debut outing in the 1983 South African Grand Prix at Johannesburg's high-altitude Kyalami circuit, more than two years after the first contact between the British F1 team and the Japanese car maker had been made. Negotiations were complex and protracted, serving as a warning to Williams that most Japanese companies like to be the dominant partner in any such business relationship. Honda started its F1 turbocharged engine programme from a very modest level indeed, and when the first of these compact little 80-degree V6 engines was delivered to the Williams factory at Didcot, Oxfordshire, it was in a box with two turbochargers. It was left for Williams to design and develop such crucial ancillaries as the radiators and exhaust system.

In the opening stages of the 1984 Portuguese Grand Prix at Estoril there was a wheel-to-wheel battle for second place between Keke Rosberg in the Williams FW09B and Nigel Mansell, the man who would be joining the team alongside him in the next season, in the black-and-gold Lotus-Renault 94T. Both eventually retired from this race but Rosberg had long since decided that if Mansell was joining Williams at the start of 1985 then he would be leaving when his contract expired at the end of that season. The chipper and confident driver from Birmingham had already attracted criticism from Rosberg earlier in 1984. After winning the Dallas Grand Prix, Keke had delivered a stinging rebuke to Mansell from the victory rostrum over what he regarded as his unacceptable driving tactics. To be fair to Rosberg, by the time he left Williams to join McLaren at the end of 1985, he accepted that he'd paid a little too much attention to F1 pit-lane gossip. Nigel hadn't proved as awkward as he'd expected and eventually he grew to like him.

It is clearly extremely difficult to be involved in F1 on an all-a[...] full-time basis and have any spare energy to expend on other t[...] projects. However, Williams made an exception in 1981 when [...] approached to engineer the Metro 6R4 rally car, an evolved ve[...] of which is seen here kicking up the dirt in the hands of Tony [...] and Rob Arthur on their way to becoming 1985 British Cham[...] Rover competition chief John Davenport asked Williams whe[...] would be possible to squeeze a Rover V6 engine into the tiny [...] hatchback. Eventually this was managed by the expedient of p[...] the engine at the rear of the Metro and adopting a four-wheel-[...] system, following the example set by the Audi Quattro which [...] enjoying huge rally success at the time. Rover accepted Willia[...] design suggestion and the team delivered three prototypes to [...] in November 1981. The car would become the mainstay of G[...] rallying throughout the mid-1980s.

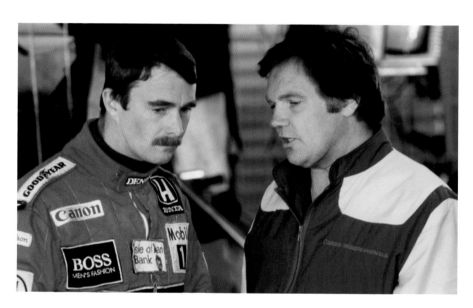

Nigel Mansell with Patrick Head during the 1985 season. When Nigel joined the Williams team he was thirty years old, had been racing in F1 with Lotus for over four seasons . . . and never once won a race. Frank Williams thought long and hard before finally committing to him, frankly believing that he was signing up a strong, determined number two to Rosberg who might occasionally win a race while regularly scoring points. Mansell may have been cast in the role of a moaner by many people in the Grand Prix paddocks, but Williams and Head found him to be quite straightforward and tolerable on their first acquaintance. His first outing for the team came at Donington Park towards the end of 1984 when he tested the FW09B, a car that had also gained itself something of an unloved reputation. Yet Mansell seemed quite impressed and left with an extremely positive opinion. He was sufficiently astute to see the potential of the Williams–Honda partnership. Williams, by their own admission, took a little longer to appreciate the potential of their new recruit.

The Williams-Honda FW10 projected a sleek, wind-cheating profile compared with its immediate predecessor, the humpy and lumpy FW09B. This machine would win four Grands Prix during the course of the 1985 season – two each for Keke Rosberg and Nigel Mansell – and would mark something of a technical turning point for the team as the first Williams car to be built around a carbon-fibre composite chassis. Patrick Head was very cautious when it came to adopting this form of chassis construction, which had been first used by McLaren four years earlier. It was not that Patrick doubted the merits of this strong, light method of construction based on aerospace materials, but he was concerned with certain aspects of its impact-resistant qualities. The aluminium chassis around which previous Williams cars had been constructed had performed well in a couple of massive accidents and it was impossible to be 100 per cent sure that the carbon-fibre chassis would be as reliable. The cost of using subcontracted carbon-fibre specialists was also a concern to Head, who had always been mindful of keeping costs down to a reasonable level. In the end the team did not embark on its own carbon-fibre chassis programme until it was in a position to control the manufacturing process itself. Over the winter of 1984/5 the Honda engineers worked hard to develop their V6 engines, concentrating on making their power delivery rather less explosive when the driver jabbed the throttle with his right foot. The first race of the year (BELOW) was the Brazilian Grand Prix at Rio de Janeiro where Keke Rosberg led for the first ten laps before his Williams FW10's engine failed. This was certainly a lurid generation of Grand Prix cars and the new Williams had a six-speed gearbox in order to handle the 900 b.h.p.-plus that the Honda V6 was developing in race trim, let alone the 1000 b.h.p.-plus it could muster for short qualifying sprints. Rosberg stormed into a 2.5-second lead by the end of the opening lap and was revelling in the Williams-Honda's sheer power during the opening stages of the race, delighting the crowds with a succession of huge oversteering slides. It was a performance that certainly suggested that the team would be in with a chance in 1985. And so it proved.

Frank Williams poses between his team's two FW10 challengers in the pit lane at the Osterreichring, the spectacular circuit in the Styrian mountains which provided the venue for the Austrian Grand Prix. As fate would have it, 1985 would be Frank's final F1 season before the road accident that changed his life for ever the following spring. Before being paralysed, Frank was the physically vibrant mainspring of the team, dodging hither and thither, hustling, worrying, encouraging and cajoling his workforce on to greater efforts. He was a passionate and enthusiastic runner with the demeanour of an over-anxious whippet. It was clear that once his mobility had become restricted, Honda became extremely unconfident about his ability to run his own company. It did not seem to matter that he was surrounded by a capable team, or that in 1986 and 1987 the Williams-Hondas would be the dominant cars on the F1 scene. The accident would be the first step towards the dissolution of the team's partnership with Honda.

LEFT Keke Rosberg leads on the opening lap of the 1985 Dutch Grand Prix at Zandvoort in his Williams-Honda FW10. The race saw him start from second place on the grid alongside Nelson Piquet's Brabham-BMW. He retired from this event, leaving the McLaren-TAGs of Niki Lauda and Alain Prost to race wheel-to-wheel for victory in the closing stages of the race, Lauda winning his sole F1 victory of the 1985 season, his last. Lauda would retire at the end of the season and by the time Rosberg competed in this race he had already agreed to join McLaren as Prost's team-mate for the 1986 World Championship programme. Keke also planned that 1986 would be his final year in F1. Not so Mansell, of course. He finished sixth in the Dutch Grand Prix, but some of his best results were just around the corner.

RIGHT Keke Rosberg celebrates on the winner's rostrum after beating Ferrari drivers Stefan Johansson (left) and Michele Alboreto into second and third places in the 1985 Detroit Grand Prix. This was only Rosberg's fourth win for the team in four seasons after a characteristically gritty drive on a treacherously dusty makeshift track laid out between unyielding concrete barriers within the centre of the famous Motor City. The Detroit Grand Prix was a round of the F1 World Championship between 1982 and 1988 and was originally inaugurated by the Detroit-based US motor industry as a means of raising the city's profile and reviving its somewhat careworn city centre. Yet F1 through the streets of Detroit was never the commercial success that was hoped for and the fixture was eventually dropped from the F1 calendar.

Nigel Mansell was always a great favourite with his home crowd and had a well-established UK fan base even before he joined Williams at the start of the 1985 season. After a generally rather troubled season that included a 195 m.p.h. tyre failure during practice for the French Grand Prix at Paul Ricard, the momentum began to swing behind the British driver. In the Belgian Grand Prix at Spa-Francorchamps he posted second place to Ayrton Senna's Lotus-Renault 97T, the best result of his F1 career up to that point. But a fortnight later he delighted the crowds at Brands Hatch by winning the European Grand Prix. Here he accelerates away from the grid wheel-to-wheel with Senna's Lotus, which he eventually beat into second place. Keke Rosberg finished third ahead of Alain Prost, but the Frenchman thereby clinched his first World Championship title. Eight years later he would win his fourth at the wheel of a Williams-Renault.

BELOW It is a familiar trend: a driver waits for ages to score his first Grand Prix victory – and immediately wins again soon afterwards. So it was for Nigel Mansell in the closing weeks of the 1985 season. Only a fortnight after winning at Brands Hatch he again mounted the upper step of the winner's rostrum at the end of the South African Grand Prix, where he was joined by Rosberg, who'd finished second. Keke had been running ahead of Mansell when he'd been the first driver to skid on oil dropped by another competitor. There were no warning flags and Keke slid off the track, handing the advantage to his team-mate. Rosberg was understandably not amused by this misfortune and set a new lap record at over 134 m.p.h. as he battled to get back on terms with Mansell, taking the chequered flag just over seven seconds behind him.

RIGHT Keke Rosberg rounded off his association with the team on the best possible note by winning the 1985 Australian Grand Prix at Adelaide's splendidly configured Victoria Park circuit. This was the first time that Australia had been represented on the F1 World Championship calendar, twenty-nine years after Stirling Moss had driven his Maserati 250F there during a non-championship fixture that celebrated Melbourne hosting the 1956 Olympic Games. Mansell understandably went into this race aiming for a hat-trick of victories and looked strong throughout qualifying, lining up alongside Ayrton Senna's pole-position Lotus-Renault. He got away first, but midway round the opening lap Senna dived down the inside, forcing Mansell wide on to the outfield. He retired with technical problems and Rosberg enjoyed a well-judged tactical run to score the fifth and final Grand Prix win of his career. He is shown here on the rostrum together with Ligier drivers Jacques Laffite (left) and Philippe Streiff, who finished second and third.

Nelson Piquet was recruited to drive for the team on a two-year contract from the start of the 1986 season, sparking the most intense intra-team rivalry Frank's team has probably ever experienced. Piquet arrived at Williams as a two-time World Champion, having won the title driving for the Bernie Ecclestone-owned Brabham team in 1981 and 1983. Mindful of how the team had been left in the lurch by Alan Jones's retirement announcement late in 1981, Williams was not about to get caught out a second time. Frank did the deal to sign Piquet on the day prior to the 1985 Austrian Grand Prix. By then, of course, Nigel Mansell had not established his winning pedigree. Yet, by the time Piquet drove his first race for Williams the following year, it was beyond question that Nigel was maturing into a formidable contender in his own right. The tension between the two men would crackle like static electricity. Piquet believed he'd been signed as number-one driver and that this guaranteed him priority over the second driver. In that he was certainly mistaken.

Mansell featured in the closest finish in F1 history when his Williams-Honda FW11 just lost this sprint to the finishing line against Ayrton Senna's Lotus 98T in the first Spanish Grand Prix to be held at the new circuit at Jerez de la Frontera. This was a marginal race for the fuel consumption of all contemporary F1 cars as the maximum fuel capacity had been slashed at the start of the season from 220 to 195 litres. Mansell had dropped as low as fifth early in the race, anxious to conserve his fuel load, but he gradually worked his way through to the lead, getting ahead of Senna after neatly boxing him in behind Martin Brundle's Tyrrell as they lapped the slower car. Once ahead, Mansell quickly opened up a decisive lead, but a slow puncture and a slight problem with the aerodynamic diffuser under the rear of the car working loose meant that he pitted for fresh tyres with a handful of laps to go. He just failed to catch the Lotus by one-hundredth of a second.

For much of the 1986 season the Williams-Honda FW11s proved to be the class of the F1 field, but at Monaco it was the rival McLarens which dominated. Alain Prost started from pole position and ran to an unchallenged victory ahead of his team-mate, former Williams teamster Keke Rosberg. Ayrton Senna's Lotus 98T finished third with Mansell (LEFT) – who'd started alongside Prost on the front row of the grid – fourth, the final runner not to be lapped by the victorious Frenchman's McLaren-TAG. Monaco would always be an unlucky race for Mansell. In 1984 he'd been pulling away from the field when he spun off in his Lotus, and in 1992 a late pit stop to check for a possible deflating rear tyre dropped him behind Senna's victorious McLaren into second place.

The rivalry between Nigel Mansell and Nelson Piquet was accentuated by the sheer speed of the Williams-Hondas throughout 1986. The personal battle between the two men was thrown into graphic focus during the British Grand Prix at Brands Hatch. Here Piquet leads Mansell as they plunge down Paddock Bend during their race-long battle that was eventually resolved when the Brazilian ace missed a gear as he changed up from fourth on one of the fastest sections of the Kent circuit. In a split second Mansell was alongside him, then through and into the lead. It was Mansell's second win at Brands Hatch in just over eight months, having won the previous year's European Grand Prix, and consolidated his popularity among the wildly enthusiastic capacity crowd. If 'Mansell mania' hadn't been triggered the previous autumn, his success in the British Grand Prix proved that it had definitely arrived. And was here to stay for many years.

During the second half of the 1986 season the Williams-Honda advantage seemed to swing subtly in Nelson Piquet's direction. The Brazilian had opened the year by winning his home Grand Prix at Rio de Janeiro where he'd been hard pressed to conceal his mirth after Mansell crashed out early in the race while battling Ayrton Senna's Lotus-Renault. Yet as the two men got into the swing of the season, Mansell emerged as the more consistent – some would say convincing – performer. At Hockenheim, however, Piquet, seen here celebrating his success, at least stemmed the tide with a commanding fifteen-second victory over Senna while Mansell trailed home a distant third. Piquet would win two of the next three races, dominating the Hungarian and Italian Grands Prix, although both drivers failed to make it to the finish of the Austrian Grand Prix at the Osterreichring.

Nigel Mansell storms round the Osterreichring during the 1986 Austrian Grand Prix, a race from which he would retire with a broken driveshaft. By this stage in the season there was certainly no doubt that Mansell had matured into a credible and highly rated World Championship contender. His terrific speed, particularly in testing, inevitably provided a terrific motivational force for the mechanics who were all impressed with the depth of his commitment each time he climbed into the cockpit. By contrast, Piquet's approach was less overtly spectacular. The Brazilian was perhaps less concerned about the egotistical need to be quick in each and every test session, taking a more measured and strategic approach to his pre-race preparations. Nelson would run all day at a test with a heavy fuel load, knowing that he was doing valuable homework in preparation for the next race; knowing full well that, when the starting signal was given, he would be in pretty good shape. By contrast, Mansell was very much a driver who wore his heart on his sleeve.

The World Championship contenders: from left, Ayrton Senna, Alain Prost and Williams-Honda team-mates Nigel Mansell and Nelson Piquet put on brave and fraternal faces for the camera at Adelaide prior to the 1986 Australian Grand Prix. This was the remarkable race in which Mansell's Williams suffered a 200 m.p.h. tyre failure while running in second place to Piquet, a position which would have ensured the British driver of the World Championship had he sustained it through to the chequered flag.

In the aftermath of Mansell's retirement following that failure, it was deemed prudent to call in Piquet for a precautionary tyre change. He resumed in second place but was unable to catch Prost, who stormed away to his second successive championship crown, the first back-to-back title holder since Jack Brabham in 1960.

Nelson Piquet scored an impressive victory in the 1986 Italian Grand Prix at Monza, beating Nigel Mansell by 9.8 seconds over the course of the 51-lap, 183-mile race. The rival Benetton-BMW team had secured pole position with a remarkable lap from Italian driver Teo Fabi at an average speed of 154.312 m.p.h. After this race – and with just three rounds of the title chase to go – Mansell led the World Championship points table on 61 ahead of Piquet (56), Alain Prost (53) and Ayrton Senna (48). Piquet by this stage was convinced that the team management should intervene to emphasise his claim to team leadership. But the management – racers to their very core – continued to feel that, having provided absolutely top-line equipment for both drivers, the best man should win. To his credit, Nelson Piquet never felt that he could bother Frank himself with these problems, given the personal struggle his team boss was currently undergoing. Yet they would resurface, with added recriminations, in 1987.

Murray Walker, the British television commentator, tries a Williams-Honda FW11 for size at Estoril in 1986. Walker is flanked by team drivers Nelson Piquet and Nigel Mansell with (right) Frank Williams, now wheelchair bound but looking extremely tanned and healthy only a few months after the road accident that resulted in his disability. Walker was always a passionate supporter of the Williams team and did much to boost the level of British public interest in the F1 business after Mansell joined the Didcot-based team in 1985. It would certainly have been good for business had Mansell managed to win the title that year. It had been eleven years since the last British driver, James Hunt, had been crowned champion. In the event we would have to wait another six years before Mansell took the title, back at the wheel of a Williams-Renault.

Nigel Mansell started the 1987 World Championship season brimful of confidence. In his third season with the Williams-Honda squad he was still nominally number-two driver to Piquet, although in reality the only material advantage this gave the Brazilian driver was priority access to the spare Williams FW11B, a refined development of the previous year's car that had at least won the 1986 Constructors' World Championship. Superficially, Williams's partnership with Honda looked as strong and secure as ever, but in reality there were some ominous straws in the wind that would eventually jeopardise Mansell's position as an F1 front runner. Piquet, for one, was very shrewd when it came to cultivating the Honda top brass and key engineers, and a hint of the Japanese company's future strategy could be seen in the decision to supply the rival Lotus team with Honda engines from the start of the season. So the dynamic Ayrton Senna, one of Nigel's most formidable rivals, now found a niche within the Honda domain. It was a development that would have far-reaching consequences for both Mansell and the team management.

The 1987 Detroit Grand Prix saw Mansell accelerate into an immediate lead in his Williams-Honda FW11B, only to drop back through the pack to an eventual fifth. His fading form was blamed on painful leg cramps which made it extremely difficult to press the pedals effectively, yet with typical determination he pressed on to finish the race. Nelson Piquet finished second on this occasion and the race was won by Ayrton Senna in the Lotus-Honda 99T, the last Grand Prix to be won by the legendary British marque, which faded from the F1 front rank over the next few seasons. Yet even as Senna took the chequered flag, negotiations were going on behind the scenes to guarantee him a place with the top-flight McLaren team in 1988. They would also see McLaren concluding a deal to use Honda engines. The breach between Williams and Honda was now only weeks away.

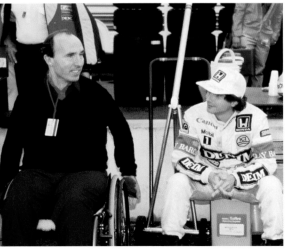

Nelson Piquet with Frank Williams in the summer of 1987. It was destined to be a troubled season for both men. Piquet would win his third World Championship on the strength of three race wins and a number of consistent points-scoring top-six finishes. Mansell won six races but lost out in his battle for the title for a second successive year. Piquet's fans believed that their man took a deliberately conservative approach to the year, confident in the belief that Mansell's impulsive streak would trip him up on a number of occasions. This is a theory that doesn't quite bear detailed analysis. In fairness, any assessment of Piquet's season must take into account the fact that for much of the year he was suffering from the after-effects of a big accident during practice for the San Marino Grand Prix at Imola, which was almost certainly caused by a tyre failure. Frank Dernie, Piquet's race engineer throughout the season, concluded that the accident affected his long-term driving capability, most notably at Monaco where he drove an unspectacular race to finish second, beaten by Ayrton Senna's demonstrably inferior Lotus 99T.

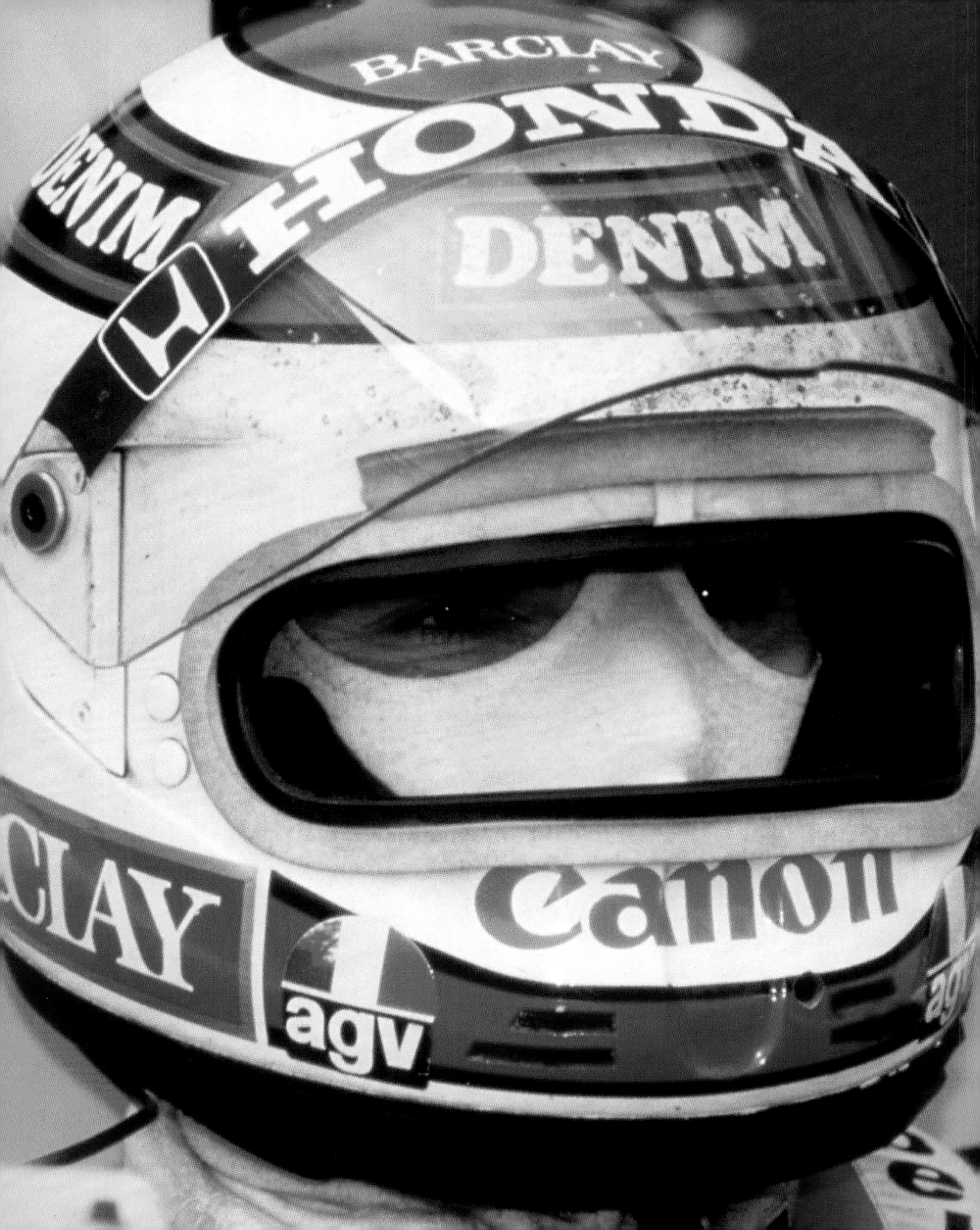
BARCLAY
DENIM
DENIM
canon
agv

LEFT Nelson Piquet celebrates victory in the 1987 German Grand Prix flanked by Ferrari's second-place Stefan Johansson (left) and Ayrton Senna, who finished third in the Lotus-Honda. Amazingly, this was the eighth round of the championship and the occasion of Piquet's first win of the season. Up to that point he had finished second on five occasions, once to Alain Prost and twice each to Senna and his own team-mate Nigel Mansell. This was the start of a promising run, however, as three more wins and two more second places lay ahead of him over the balance of the season as he confidently consolidated his edge. It says much for the team's underlying even-handedness and sense of fair play that, even though he told Frank Williams on the evening prior to the Hungarian Grand Prix on 16 August that he would be switching to Lotus the following year, there was never any hint of partiality against his efforts. Three weeks later, at the Italian Grand Prix, Honda would announce they were terminating their contract with Williams, despite the fact that it still had a year to run.

LEFT Nelson Piquet at the wheel of the sleek Williams-Honda FW11B. The Brazilian driver gained enormous personal satisfaction from working away behind the scenes at a technical development that would enable him to go to a Grand Prix starting grid confident that he would enjoy a decisive performance edge. The way in which he harnessed the Williams team's resources to get the best out of its newly developed, computer-controlled reactive suspension in the 1987 Italian Grand Prix at Monza was a case in point. Prior to the race Nelson completed a simulated race distance test at Imola, taking over a minute off Mansell's race-winning time established earlier in the season at the San Marino Grand Prix. He used it at Monza to win, beating Senna's Lotus-Honda into second place. By then, of course, Piquet had committed himself to Lotus for the following season. 'Williams were technically the best team I ever worked with,' he reflected. 'But I didn't join them to compete with a team-mate who made it difficult for me to win races.'

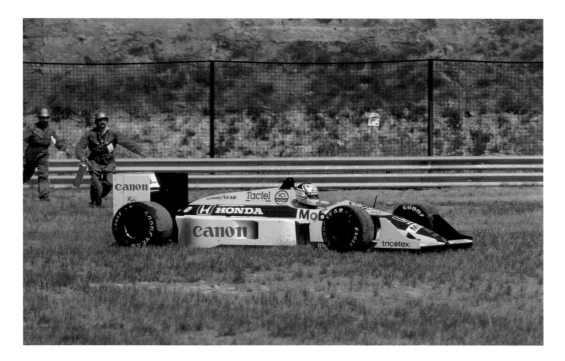

ABOVE Formula One racing can be a capricious and unpredictable business at the best of times, but few disappointments can have matched that experienced by Nigel Mansell while leading the 1987 Hungarian Grand Prix at the Hungaroring. The right rear wheel-securing nut on his Williams-Honda FW11B gradually unwound itself and flew off, leaving Mansell to pull gingerly on to the grass and brake the car to a standstill before the wheel came off completely. It was a bitterly disappointing outcome for the British driver, particularly as Piquet was the beneficiary of his disappointment and went on to win the race. Had Mansell survived to the finish it might have made a crucial difference to his World Championship tally. All else being equal, a win in Hungary would have seen him dead-heat on 71 points with Piquet, thereby clinching the title on the basis of more race wins than his rival.

Nigel Mansell storms to victory in the 1987 Mexican Grand Prix at the punishingly bumpy Autodromo Hermanos Rodriguez, one of the most demanding and spectacular circuits to have been included in the F1 World Championship schedule in recent years. Piquet finished second in this, the final race to be won by Mansell in a Honda-powered Williams, and the chasm of distrust and hostility between the two drivers had seldom been wider. The race was stopped and restarted following an accident involving Derek Warwick's Arrows-Megatron, the two parts of the race being aggregated for the final result. At the restart Piquet got away ahead, but as he had to make up forty-five seconds on Mansell one might have expected the Englishman simply to sit on his tail all the way to the finish. But that was certainly not Mansell's style. He attempted to overtake Piquet, but Nelson closed the door on him. The two men would have much to say about this episode later in the day. Piquet was first past the chequered flag on the road, but Mansell was the winner by just over twenty-six seconds.

The end of the road for Nigel Mansell's 1987 title chances finally came during the first qualifying session for the Japanese Grand Prix at Suzuka when he crashed his Williams-Honda FW11B backwards into a tyre barrier. As the car was retrieved on the back of a truck Mansell was taken straight to the circuit medical centre from whence an emergency helicopter whisked him to the University Clinic in nearby Nagoya. Initially badly winded, Mansell had suffered severe bruising, muscular strain and shock in the high-speed impact and was forbidden on medical grounds from taking any further part in the Japanese Grand Prix weekend. He was kept in hospital for observation overnight and then boarded a flight to return to Europe the following day.

The consequences of the accident also caused him to miss the final race of the season in Adelaide a fortnight later. The Japanese race proved to be a bad day for Honda on its home track, for although Piquet clinched the World Championship he failed to finish due to a rare engine failure.

Nigel Mansell's absence from the 1987 Australian Grand Prix allowed Williams the chance to give Riccardo Patrese a try-out in preparation for his joining the team the following year. The pleasant Italian had earlier tested a Williams-Honda at Imola and was released to drive in Adelaide by Brabham team chief Bernie Ecclestone, for whom he'd first driven in 1982. Bernie was keen to ensure Patrese a continued place on the F1 grid in the wake of BMW's withdrawal as engine supplier to the Brabham team. Despite experiencing a multitude of minor mechanical glitches, Patrese managed to qualify seventh, just 0.7 seconds behind Piquet's time, which had earned him third place on the grid. In the race he held fourth place in the closing stages only to retire with engine failure just six laps from the end of the eighty-two-lap race. Piquet also failed to finish, rounding off his career as a Williams driver on a sorely disappointing note.

ABOVE Riccardo Patrese (right), Nigel Mansell and the rest of the team personnel with the Williams-Judd FW12 at the start of the 1988 World Championship season. The Honda engine contract was now a memory and the team certainly seemed to have a struggle on its hands, even though the prospect of using the naturally aspirated Judd 3.5-litre V10 engine against a new generation of further detuned turbocharged engines looked like a reasonable project from the start of the year. The feeling was that a light and agile machine such as the FW12 would give the turbos a run for their money before they were phased out completely at the end of 1988. The year started well, with Mansell qualifying strongly on the front row of the grid for the Brazilian Grand Prix at Rio, but thereafter little of the potential was realised.

RIGHT Nigel Mansell with Williams technical director Patrick Head (centre) and race engineer David Brown. This was Mansell's fourth season with the team and he'd originally signed up believing that he would be racing with Honda engines through to the end of 1988. Frank Williams was impressed with the way he handled the obvious disappointment, feeling that the trials and tribulations of 1988 left Mansell much better equipped to handle the setbacks that are part and parcel of the F1 game. Mansell's contract did not say he could leave if there was no Honda engine contract in place, but Williams recalled approvingly that this was hardly the point: Nigel never tried to leave. He was vocal in his disappointment as the season unfolded, but his loyalty to the team was certainly beyond question.

Mansell's Williams-Judd FW12 is briefly halted by flag marshals at the end of the pit lane at the Circuit Paul Ricard, near Bandol, which was the venue for the 1988 French Grand Prix. In this race Mansell recorded his seventh successive retirement, this time with a problem in the computer-controlled reactive suspension system. Although this suspension arrangement had displayed undeniable promise towards the end of the previous season when installed on a Williams-Honda FW11B, it was proving to be more trouble than it was worth on the FW12. Things came to a head over the British Grand Prix weekend and the car was rebuilt before the race with a more conventional springing system. Come the race, Mansell simply flew through the field in unpredictable wet/dry track conditions to finish second behind Ayrton Senna's victorious McLaren-Honda MP4/4.

Just two days before the start of practice for the 1988 Belgian Grand Prix, Martin Brundle was cruising up the M11 in his Jaguar Sovereign, bound for his home in Kings Lynn, when the carphone rang and Frank Williams offered him the role of Nigel Mansell's understudy for this challenging eleventh round of the World Championship. Earlier in the season Martin had impressed Patrick Head with his testing performances in the reactive-suspension Williams FW12 and so he seemed the logical choice for this race. Martin did a good job: he was quicker than Patrese in Friday's free practice session, lined up twelfth on the grid and posted fastest time in one wet qualifying session. In the race he finished ninth after slightly overtaxing his tyres in the early stages of the race. It was a performance that put Brundle back in the frame as a potential full-time F1 competitor.

profile

Patrick Head

'Are you prepared to work twenty-four hours a day to achieve success in Formula One?' The scene was the lounge of a swanky London hotel, the man asking the question F1 team chief Frank Williams. It was late 1975 and Frank was interviewing for the post of chief designer at his financially strapped company Frank Williams (Racing Cars) Limited. The reply from the young candidate marked him as a little out of the ordinary. 'I am certainly not,' replied Patrick Head. 'Because anybody who has to do that must be extremely disorganised.' He got the job.

Life with Williams in those days was always unpredictable. Almost as soon as Head took up his post Frank's company was transformed into Walter Wolf Racing when he sold a controlling interest to the Austro-Canadian oil man. Inevitably, working for somebody else in a management role didn't appeal to Williams. In 1977 he decided to establish his own serious Formula One team. He bought a second-hand March 761 and established Williams Grand Prix Engineering – and Patrick Head went with him as its chief designer. A generation later, Patrick continues to preside over the engineering side of what has become the third most successful F1 team of all time, trailing only Ferrari and McLaren in the all-time Grand Prix winners' stakes. More significantly, the Frank and Patrick show represents the longest relationship between designer and team principal in motor-racing history.

Patrick started in the motor-racing business with an honours degree from London University. He also raced clubmans sports cars in British events, which gave him some insight into the mind of the racing driver. After joining Williams he quickly forged a reputation as a practical

and cautious engineer. 'In the early part of my career I got cured of any idea of being egotistical from an engineering standpoint,' he says. 'By that I mean in the sense that one might say, "I'm going to prove to the world that my conceptual ideas are better than anybody else's." I think that attitude came about because I saw the damage that can be done to a company if one person overindulges himself in conceptual ideas that do not work.'

Patrick is particularly mindful of the problems that befell Lotus founder Colin Chapman in 1979. After designing the revolutionary ground-effect Lotus 79 the previous year, Chapman tried to develop the concept one stage further, only for the Lotus 80 to prove a complete failure. 'Chapman was such a big figure at Lotus, in complete charge and with an enormous reputation, that he could take a risk like that,' Patrick explains. 'That car went through 1979 with bits falling off it for much of the time, which is why Carlos Reutemann came to drive for us. But while Lotus could arguably afford to take time off for such experiments, if we had endured a year like that, certainly in our early days, we would have been hard pressed to survive. Granted, we had bad years like 1984, but we always managed to produce sufficient expectation for the following season. So I learned early on that you've got to do a good, solid job to survive and keep your credibility in this business.'

Head, at fifty-five years old much trimmer and more youthful than one might expect from anybody who's had to work with dear old Frank for two decades, possesses the sort of personality that tends to disarm people. He is straightforward and has a down-to-earth approach to motor racing. It's often been said that Williams is primarily an engineering company whose specialist activity is Grand Prix racing. That probably wouldn't be the case for Frank, the ultimate racer's racer, but the concept probably comes close to mirroring Patrick's commitment to engineering excellence.

Patrick certainly has a well-developed understanding of what gives the team its distinctive character and identity: 'Frank's enthusiasm for what he does hasn't changed since his accident, and that enthusiasm is transmitted to all the people in the company,' he says. 'Frank makes himself present throughout the company, so during the course of a week he'll come into contact with nearly everybody. I think continuity is another key factor. Frank and I have been together for a long time and I think the workforce understands our wishes. They know that we want Williams to be a viable business so that it can grow and strengthen itself. It isn't a vehicle simply to provide Frank and I with a good living, although, thanks to Bernie, thanks to people who switch on their TVs and push the business on, it has become a sound business. But equally, if you don't run your company well, and if you're not successful, it's quite easy to get into a position where the numbers don't add up. I think the main things are enthusiasm from the top and clarity of ownership of the company. Both Frank and I are fairly pragmatic people and that must come through, I suppose.'

Patrick has been crucial to the team's success over the last twenty-five years, but typically plays down his role in the development of the sport as a whole. 'I think, in general terms, the sport has changed quite a lot largely because of the very impressive increase in engine power. We're now running into the highest levels in race trim of the turbo era; meanwhile, the cars have had to be pegged back enormously in terms of performance. Personally, I would have liked to see slightly less restriction on the cars and slightly more on the engines. But that hasn't happened and we've obviously had to respond to what has happened.'

With that in mind, does he miss the challenge of developing such concepts as four-wheel drive, active suspension and constantly variable transmission – all aspects of racing-car design tackled by Williams over the past couple of decades? 'Yes, obviously, as an engineer,' he admits. 'To me, the engineering function is the most important thing. However, this question is part of a wider debate in deciding what's best for Formula One and whether there should be such freedom in the rules that makes the technical content more important than the driver. I have to say, as a motorsport enthusiast, rather than as an engineer, I don't think it is appropriate that drivers should have anti-lock braking so that they can just stand on the pedal as hard as they like at all times, regardless of whether there's oil or water on the track, and the electronics just sort it all out. I don't think it's appropriate that they should have a steering system that corrects before the driver can for incipient oversteer, or whatever, and I think it is right that these things are not allowed. Yet, as an engineer, I have to say these things are very interesting. Technology is technology, and it's up to motor racing to harness it to best effect.'

On the topic of Williams drivers over the years, if he has contentious views about some of the sport's top achievers, he keeps them concealed behind a wry grin. 'Let's just say that they were all different and all had strongly different personalities, and it's quite a challenge from time to time. Sometimes if you think a driver is not making the best of his capabilities, you can pass a bit of advice across. But most of the time they're pretty independent, self-controlling people.'

The major change Patrick has seen over his quarter-century in the sport is the growth of specialist areas in the development of F1 engineering, something that has put at a premium the company's organisational and administrative skills. This process of evolution has, out of necessity, prompted Patrick to adopt a more selective approach to the way the team operates. 'I like either myself or our engineers to come up with interesting ideas or interesting solutions to technical problems, and to follow them through with good logic and consistency until they're successful on the track,' he says. 'That's what I get the greatest buzz from. At the track I think there are so many ways of doing it wrong that I'm always very concerned that we don't, of our own volition, choose one of those ways. That's quite difficult both in the run-up to the race and once the race has started.'

RIGHT On the rostrum at Silverstone at the end of the 1988 British Grand Prix, Mansell celebrates his great run to second place. It would be the highlight of an otherwise largely fruitless season in which he managed to finish second on one other occasion, in the Spanish Grand Prix at Jerez. Mansell also shone in the Hungarian Grand Prix at the tortuous Hungaroring, shadowing Ayrton Senna's McLaren-Honda for many laps before getting too close to his rival, losing downforce and spinning off the circuit. In the aftermath of this race Mansell was struck down by a virulent attack of chickenpox which prevented him from contesting either the Belgian Grand Prix at Spa-Francorchamps or the Italian Grand Prix at Monza. His stand-ins for those two races were respectively Martin Brundle and Jean-Louis Schlesser.

LEFT Riccardo Patrese exits the pit lane at Monza during practice for the 1988 Italian Grand Prix, the driver from Padua about to accelerate out on to the huge start/finish apron which so dominates the area in front of the pits at this famous circuit. Riccardo would finish seventh in this race, which saw a memorable Ferrari one–two for Gerhard Berger and Michele Alboreto, barely a month after the death of the legendary Italian team's founder Enzo Ferrari. Patrese's team-mate for the weekend, F1 novice Jean-Louis Schlesser, had helped the Ferrari team on its way to that unexpected success, accidentally tripping up leader Ayrton Senna's McLaren-Honda as the Brazilian driver lapped him in the closing stages of the race.

Jean-Louis Schlesser was a member of the Sauber-Mercedes sports car team and had tested for Williams in the past. He ran at a modest pace on the high-speed Monza circuit and was holding eleventh place – and about to be lapped for the second time – when Senna came on to his tail going into the penultimate lap of the race. On this rare occasion Ayrton's aggressive overtaking style got the better of him. Schlesser drove on to the dirt and locked up as Senna braked inside the Williams, Ayrton clearly thinking that the slower car would run wide out of the corner. Instead, the two cars collided. Schlesser and Senna discussed the matter after the race in a cool, controlled and formally polite fashion. Schlesser very firmly expressed his regret over the incident, but equally firmly declined to accept responsibility for it.

End of an era, for the moment, at least. Riccardo Patrese heads towards fourth place in the 1988 Australian Grand Prix at Adelaide ahead of team-mate Nigel Mansell, who would retire from the race following an accident caused by slight brake problems. By this time Mansell was on course to join Ferrari the following season as team-mate to Gerhard Berger. It would turn out to be a turbulent and often controversial two-year stint with the Italian team. Patrese, meanwhile, would stay on in the Williams camp. He would still be there when Mansell decided to rejoin the team at the start of 1991, by which time a new era had begun thanks to a long-term engine-supply partnership with Renault, the French car maker.

CHAPTER THREE

A New Partnership with Renault

The start of the 1989 season marked a new dawn for the Williams team barely sixteen months after splitting with Honda. Mindful that the escalating cost and complexity of contemporary F1 placed a premium on a close association with an engine manufacturer, Frank and Patrick concluded a long-term deal with Renault. For the 1989 season the team commenced a new partnership with Renault, using their newly developed 3.5-litre V10 engine in the first season of the post-turbo era. This was very much a learning year for both members of this Anglo-French alliance, but the signs were promising, and Thierry Boutsen won two races for the team.

In 1990 the partnership progressed slowly, with Patrese and Boutsen scoring a victory apiece, but the team raised its game dramatically in 1991 with the new Williams FW14, which would be driven by Patrese and celebrated returnee Nigel Mansell. Williams was certainly aiming high at this point in its history, determined to bring to an end a four-year stranglehold on the World Championship by the rival McLaren-Honda squad.

By this stage in the team's history not only was aerodynamic research developing dramatically, but computer-aided design and manufacturing (CAD/CAM) facilities were becoming essential for them, as for all top F1 operations. Such systems enabled designers to view a three-dimensional image of the proposed chassis layout on a computer screen and then experiment with various details without having to cut metal or carbon-fibre to make prototype components. For checking such crucial subtleties as radiator ducts, or deciding on the merits of a new rear wing, the installation of CAD/CAM systems would contribute to a much more economical use of an engineer's time.

1989–91

The new alliance had its roots in a meeting between Frank, Patrick and key personnel from Renault Sport over the weekend of the 1987 Portuguese Grand Prix. Renault had been out of the F1 arena since the end of 1986, but chief engineer Bernard Dudot had kept well in touch with evolving developments and a small group of engineers duly worked away on a new V10 engine to comply with the 3.5-litre naturally aspirated regulations. This 67-degree unit would be used by Williams from the start of the 1989 season and a float of some thirty engines was built up by the middle of the season to service the requirements of the two-car team. The Renault V10 was initially intended to be installed in a brand-new Williams chassis from the start of the 1989 season, but Patrick Head eventually had second thoughts and concluded that there was still more potential to be unlocked from the FW12 design that had been powered by the Judd V8 engine throughout the previous season. The resultant FW12C (BELOW) was very much a development chassis that served the team well as they got to grips with the challenge of mating the new Renault engine with the Williams transverse-mounted six-speed gearbox that had debuted in the previous year. After a season grappling with the problems of the Judd engine's oil consumption and the troublesome reactive suspension system, Patrick admitted that it was something of a relief to get back into a relationship with a major car manufacturer. The first of the Williams-Renault FW12s ran at Paul Ricard in October 1988 with Riccardo Patrese at the wheel.

ABOVE RIGHT The race bay at the Williams team's headquarters at Basil Hill Road, Didcot, to which the company moved in June 1984, the original facilities on the Station Road Industrial Estate by this stage bursting at the

seams as the company ramped up its partnership with engine partners Honda. Throughout the 1980s and into the next decade the tempo of F1 technical development would accelerate dramatically, requiring more space for a bigger workforce, more sophisticated machinery and much ancillary equipment such as an on-site wind tunnel. Williams would remain at these premises from 1984 to 1996, when the need for further expansion prompted a move to even bigger premises at Grove, near Wantage, about twelve miles further to the west.

Nominating a successor to Nigel Mansell in the Williams F1 line-up was always going to be a challenge. In the event Frank opted for thirty-year-old Thierry Boutsen, a mild-mannered and calm Belgian driver who had made his F1 debut in 1983 at the wheel of an Arrows. Three more seasons with Arrows and a couple of years with the Benetton-Ford squad had earned the likeable Boutsen a respected reputation and there were many people in the F1 pit lane who had a high regard for his talents. Frank was one of them, offering Thierry a two-year contract. Yet the newcomer never quite managed to kindle an inspirational spark at Williams, an early-season testing accident at Rio perhaps contributing to the lack of obvious flair that the team had come to expect from its number-one drivers. That said, Boutsen would win two Grands Prix for Williams in 1989, both in torrential rain, both in superb style.

Thierry Boutsen has his first test at the wheel of the Williams-Renault FW12C at Jerez, southern Spain, late in 1988. Boutsen's arrival in the team allowed Riccardo Patrese to emerge from Nigel Mansell's shadow and consolidate his reputation as a truly rounded and mature F1 contestant. Both men shared the testing duties over the winter of 1988/9 but even before the season began team insiders began to realise that Patrese was the more convincing performer of the two. It would be difficult to conclude that Boutsen did anything wrong during his first season with Williams, but his driving style reflected his character too closely, being consistent, unruffled and precise. Patrese, in contrast, radiated aggression and determination, but would have to wait until 1990 before scoring his first win in a Williams.

RIGHT The 1989 Formula One season included a new US fixture run on a makeshift circuit through the streets of Phoenix, Arizona. It was a track that called for considerable precision and control and the race was won by Alain Prost's McLaren-Honda with Riccardo Patrese's Williams a strong second just 39 seconds behind after 75 gruelling laps of this 2.36-mile circuit in sweltering dry heat. Here Patrese works hard to keep ahead of his one-time kart-racing rival Eddie Cheever, whose Arrows-Ford A11 finished third, just three seconds behind the Williams. This was Riccardo's second runner-up finish in as many weeks, having followed Ayrton Senna's winning McLaren-Honda past the chequered flag in the Mexican Grand Prix the previous weekend. Cheever told Riccardo that if it hadn't been for a brake balance problem on his Arrows, he was confident that he'd have overtaken the Williams.

LEFT Midway through the 1989 Canadian Grand Prix at Montreal it seemed that the best Thierry Boutsen could hope for was a waterlogged third place in his Williams-Renault FW12C. With forty of the race's sixty-nine laps to run Ayrton Senna seemed to be speedboating his way to a commanding win, while the other Williams driven by Riccardo Patrese was holding an apparently secure second place. Boutsen was even counting his blessings: he'd lost time in the pits during a tyre change while a jammed wheel nut was sorted out; then he survived a high-speed spin without hitting anything. Yet the cards would dramatically fall in his favour. A loose undertray slowed Patrese, so Boutsen moved into second place with just six laps to go. Then Senna's Honda engine blew up spectacularly with three laps left. And Boutsen won. It was a classic demonstration of F1's oldest adage: to finish first, first you've got to finish.

LEFT A delighted Boutsen celebrates his tremendous Canadian victory at the rain-soaked Circuit Gilles Villeneuve, flanked by second and third placemen Riccardo Patrese and Andrea de Cesaris, who drove a fine race in his Scuderia Italia Dallara-Ford. Boutsen had been shaded by Patrese during practice and qualifying, the Belgian lining up sixth on the grid, two places behind his Italian team-mate. Yet he had kept his nerve and not been ruffled by the dreadful weather conditions of that afternoon and drove a superbly controlled race, aided only by a welcome slice of good fortune in the closing stages. Thierry later admitted that he didn't believe it when he came past the Williams pit and saw 'P1' on his signalling board. 'Next time round and it was still there,' he said. 'I became petrified. Every lap was crash or win after that. I just kept thinking of all the things which could go wrong.' Nothing did.

BELOW Thierry Boutsen leads team-mate Riccardo Patrese during the 1989 British Grand Prix at Silverstone, one of the more disappointing races for the Williams-Renault FW12Cs after the two drivers had qualified seventh and fifth on the grid, respectively. The British crowd were cheering Nigel Mansell's Ferrari-mounted pursuit of Alain Prost's eventually victorious McLaren-Honda as the two Williams drivers dropped away tamely from the leaders in the opening stages of the chase. Thierry had been wrestling without an operative clutch from early in the race, allowing Patrese to overtake and pull away in third place on lap sixteen. Three laps later the Italian spun off hard into the tyre barrier at Club Corner after a radiator had punctured, spewing coolant over the left rear tyre. Boutsen finished a distant tenth, two laps behind the winning McLaren, after an unscheduled pit stop to change a punctured tyre.

LEFT If Thierry Boutsen's performance in winning the 1989 Canadian Grand Prix was impressive, his victory in the same year's Australian race at Adelaide proved momentous. The track may have been wet in Montreal, but prior to the start of the Australian Grand Prix there were rivers of water running across the track in the city's Victoria Park, leaving the drivers huddled in debate as to whether it was safe even to participate, let alone seriously race. All the participants would later reflect that the conditions had been far worse than anything in recent memory. Ayrton Senna's McLaren-Honda led from the start in spectacular style, but plunged into the back of Martin Brundle's Brabham-Judd – hidden from his view in the murk – after only a dozen laps, eliminating both cars. Thereafter Boutsen surged into the lead and was never headed. It was the finest drive of his F1 career.

ABOVE The Williams-Renault FW13 finally made its race debut in the 1989 Portuguese Grand Prix at Estoril. The new car was a logical development of the FW12C, built around an entirely new chassis that was much lower at the front and packaged differently with push-rod operated spring/dampers now mounted over the driver's knees. Both Patrese and Boutsen retired from this race due to a build-up of debris flicked up off the circuit into their radiator cooling ducts that caused their engines to overheat. There had also been problems during practice when the nose-cone mountings had to be strengthened after the nose box on Boutsen's car had come loose. Things went better in the car's third race, the Japanese Grand Prix at Suzuka when Boutsen (seen here) finished third behind Alessandro Nannini's winning Benetton and Patrese.

LEFT Thierry Boutsen discusses the set-up of his Williams-Renault FW13B with the team's engineers early in 1990. Starting the year on the back of his victory in Adelaide the previous autumn, Boutsen's relationship with the Williams team would sadly start to run out of steam before many races of the new season had taken place. The formal and reserved Belgian driver could sense that he was perhaps not held in the highest regard by Williams, and, despite winning the Hungarian Grand Prix at Budapest, he did not wait around to be told that there was no long-term future for him in the team. Long before the end of the year he had signed a two-year deal beginning in 1991 with the French Ligier squad. In many ways it was a sad note on which to end his two years as a Williams driver.

BELOW Boutsen heads for fifth place in the 1990 Brazilian Grand Prix at São Paulo's Interlagos circuit, lapped by Alain Prost's winning Ferrari before the end of the race. Although the FW13 had made its debut only in the previous year's Portuguese Grand Prix, Patrick Head and his design team had much work to do in order to accommodate the new 1990-spec Renault RS2 V10 engine, which sat lower in the chassis than its immediate predecessor. This involved different engine mountings, a revised cooling system and alterations to the casing for the transverse six-speed gearbox to mate up with the new engine's lower crankshaft centreline. The resultant machine was dubbed the FW13B. During the course of the season Renault Sport would make great steps in terms of power output from their V10 and by the end of the season Boutsen and Patrese were regularly competing with around 650 b.h.p. – some 70 b.h.p. more than that developed by the first Renault V10 at the start of the previous year. Such is the unobtrusive, behind-the-scenes tempo of F1 development.

ABOVE Riccardo Patrese on the winner's rostrum at Imola after a memorable victory in the 1990 San Marino Grand Prix, applauded by McLaren-Honda driver Gerhard Berger, who finished in second place. This was Patrese's first win since the 1983 South African Grand Prix, in which he was driving a Brabham-BMW. More crucially, this was a success that buried memories of his disastrous late slip in the 1983 San Marino race, when he slid off the track while leading, handing a surprise victory to Patrick Tambay's Ferrari. Berger had led that race until ten laps from the finish when Patrese slipped ahead. 'This time, as soon as I got through into the lead, all I could think about was that I must not make a mistake and throw it all away,' Patrese said. 'That feeling produced its own pressure, believe me.' Riccardo held on confidently to finish the job and it was hard not to share his tears of joy as he ascended the podium to take his place on its highest step.

The ever-popular Riccardo Patrese celebrates his 200th Grand Prix on the eve of the 1990 British race at Silverstone, although his drive would hardly turn out to be a piece of cake. Early in the race Alessandro Nannini's Benetton ran into the back of his FW13B. Soon afterwards he came into the pits for a precautionary check over and a new set of tyres, thereafter fighting back from twentieth to fifteenth before calling it a day and retiring the car. The impact from the Benetton had damaged the aerodynamic diffuser under the rear of the Williams and the resulting handling imbalance made the car feel progressively more lurid in the fast corners. Meanwhile, at the head of the field, Nigel Mansell's Ferrari had led the race only to retire with gearbox problems. Bitterly disappointed, the former Williams driver announced that he would quit at the end of the season. 'There will be no way back for me,' he insisted. But there would be: with Williams.

Thierry Boutsen on his way to second place in the 1990 British Grand Prix at Silverstone in the Williams-Renault FW13B. He qualified fourth, just 0.8 seconds away from Mansell's pole-position Ferrari, and ran a strong third in the opening stages. In the end he would benefit from Mansell's retirement and an uncharacteristic spin by Ayrton Senna to take second place, over half a minute behind Alain Prost's winning Ferrari. Senna, a close friend as well as a rival, was under four seconds further back in third place at the chequered flag. It was a heartening result, but everybody at Williams realised they had to raise the standard of their game if they were to challenge for race wins in 1991. The FW13B's biggest shortcoming was the way it degraded its tyres during the course of a race. Patrick Head and the team's aerodynamicist, Adrian Newey, would change all that with the new car they had in mind for the following season.

Thierry Boutsen takes the chequered flag to win the 1990
Hungarian Grand Prix at Budapest, his Williams-Renault FW13B
just pipping Ayrton Senna's McLaren-Honda by 0.3 seconds after
a dramatic chase that had lasted for the final thirteen laps of the
race. Boutsen started from the first pole position of his career and
Riccardo Patrese made it an all-Williams front row. Boutsen led
from start to finish, but Senna completed the opening lap sixth
from fourth on the grid and then spent the rest of the afternoon
carving his way through the pack. He got up to third by lap fifty-six
and then started hunting down Alessandro Nannini's second-place
Benetton, which itself was closing on Boutsen. On lap sixty-four,
Senna pitched Nannini off the road and into retirement, leaving a
clear track between himself and the leading Williams. Senna quickly
closed on to Boutsen's tail, but Thierry was driving with great
precision and never left a gap his rival could exploit.

Nigel Mansell returned to Williams at the start of 1991 as a much more rounded and complete driving talent after his two challenging years with Ferrari. His mercurial, sometimes aggressively competitive personality was now spiced with a welcome streak of maturity. Five years had passed since the sudden tyre failure in a Williams-Honda at Adelaide had snatched the 1986 World Championship from his grasp at the eleventh hour. He wanted that championship even more, and generally would drive the 1991 season like a title-holder in waiting. It was no surprise when Mansell emerged as the only man really capable of facing down the legendary Ayrton Senna in split-second, wheel-to-wheel combat throughout this closely fought season. He would score some impressive victories after utterly dominant individual race performances and proved he could handle the pressure with more confidence and assurance than he'd ever previously displayed. The Williams management found Mansell a demanding, exacting – sometimes exasperating – personality to deal with.

Yet there was no questioning his ability to deliver the goods. Here, he tests the first of the new Williams-Renault FW14s at Silverstone on 22 February 1991. Williams raised their game dramatically with the FW14. Aerodynamically outstanding, its sleek profile had been shaped with great attention to detail by Adrian Newey, who had employed this distinctive 'raised nose' configuration on his two earlier designs for the Leyton House team. The new Renault RS3 V10 engine eventually developed an impressive 770 b.h.p. at 14,200 r.p.m. and the car was equipped with an electro-hydraulically activated six-speed transmission. To all intents and purposes, the RS3 was a brand-new engine from Renault Sport incorporating revised bore and stroke, new cylinder heads, a revised camshaft and induction system plus a new sump and lubrication system. The FW14 was the first properly integrated car/engine package produced by the Williams–Renault partnership. It is no understatement to say that it was the start of something big.

Mansell moves to congratulate Ayrton Senna after his Williams-Renault finished second to the Brazilian driver's McLaren-Honda in the 1991 Monaco Grand Prix. Mansell qualified fifth and ran fourth for much of the race's early stages, but he gradually moved into contention after his team-mate Riccardo Patrese crashed his Williams FW14 heavily after skidding on an oil slick dropped by Stefano Modena's expiring Tyrrell-Honda. Nigel then piled on the pressure to deprive Alain Prost's Ferrari of second place with sixteen of the race's seventy-eight laps left to run. He eventually finished eighteen seconds behind Senna to record his first finish of the season. His one-time team-mate Keke Rosberg observed wryly, 'People who write off Mansell are talking short-sighted nonsense. He is performing to the maximum every time.' Rosberg, who had partnered Nigel at Williams in 1985, knew precisely what he was talking about.

The 1991 Canadian Grand Prix should have been one of Mansell's easiest victories. He'd qualified second behind team-mate Patrese, but accelerated into an immediate lead and was never headed until the final half-mile of the sixty-nine-lap race at the Circuit Gilles Villeneuve. In the closing stages Mansell had allowed his lap times to slip as he conserved his Williams-Renault, but then he suddenly posted a new lap record with four laps to run, seemingly a symbolic effort to stamp his mark on a race he'd already dominated from the outset. Into the final lap, waving to the crowd, he arrived at the hairpin at the far end of the circuit only for the engine to cut out and his car to roll to a frustrating halt at the side of the circuit. What made it worse for Mansell was that he'd handed the victory to his old rival Nelson Piquet, now driving a Benetton-Ford, who could hardly believe his luck. Mansell's error had been to let the engine revs drop too low and it died just as the transmission baulked between gears. There was insufficient electrical charge left in the system to enable the hydraulic engagement of a gear so he was unable to coax the engine back into life. By any standards, it was a painful disappointment.

ABOVE Nigel Mansell and Ayrton Senna wheel-to-wheel as they battle for second place in the 1991 Mexican Grand Prix at the Autodromo Hermanos Rodriguez. Patrese qualified on pole position, but Mansell led from the start until Riccardo forced his way through into the lead on the fifteenth lap. Thereafter Patrese drove a copybook race, but Senna simply wouldn't leave Mansell alone, his McLaren-Honda MP4/6 harrying the Williams driver at every opportunity. Yet neither man was risking too much. Both knew that they had to race with their World Championship positions in mind. Late in the race, after the Renault engineers had carefully monitored the car-to-pit telemetry on their banks of computers in the back of the garage, it was decided to tell Mansell that he could adjust the engine's fuel/air mixture to a richer setting that would permit him to counter-attack against Patrese. This was something of a relief to Patrick Head, who also hung out a signal to Mansell, warning him not to keep running the engine up against its rev limiter for fear it might break under the strain. Yet, although Mansell piled on the pressure, he was just over a second behind Patrese at the finish. RIGHT Riccardo Patrese celebrates his victory in the 1991 Mexican Grand Prix in company with Nigel Mansell, who finished second, and Ayrton Senna, who wound up third. Mansell looked ever-so-slightly strained as he put something of a brave face on his disappointment, but his mood was nothing when compared with Senna's dismay. Ayrton was sufficiently shrewd to realise that the F1 torch had now passed from McLaren to Williams and was anxious

to know what Honda – McLaren's engine partner – was going to do about it. Despite this inner acknowledgement, Senna's early-season domination meant that he emerged from this sixth round of the World Championship with 44 points, double Patrese's tally. A third World Championship looked a likely outcome for the Brazilian driver, but he knew that the writing was on the wall in the long term. 'The Williams is now very quick indeed,' said Senna. 'Its chassis is much better than ours and if we don't get some new equipment, then we're going to have real trouble on our hands during the second half of the season.' Prophetic words indeed.

Riccardo Patrese did the perfect job as Nigel Mansell's number two during the 1991 World Championship season. With Mansell having first call on the spare Williams-Renault FW14 as part of his new deal for the team, Patrese's supporting role was clearly defined from the outset. Despite this, he outqualified Nigel in the first seven races of the season, but there was no question of his making political capital out of what was, in effect, a misleading advantage. Riccardo remained content with his own role and was happy to be judged on his personal performances. His consistent display early in the season meant that he looked in a mathematically stronger position than Mansell to challenge for the championship. Unfortunately, the odd driving error and a succession of minor mechanical setbacks undermined that effort towards the end of the summer and Mansell surged ahead to finish runner-up to Senna in the title chase. It was difficult to see how Patrese could have done anything better.

The new Circuit de Nevers at Magny-Cours became the home of the French Grand Prix in 1991, and Nigel Mansell celebrated the occasion with a confident victory in the Williams-Renault FW14. Yet this was no cakewalk and the British driver twice had to battle his way ahead of Alain Prost's Ferrari 643 to regain his advantage. 'Nigel was definitely quicker than me for most of the race today,' said Prost. 'I think the result today was the correct one.' Here Mansell celebrates on the rostrum after scoring his first win at the wheel of a Williams-Renault. To his right are Prost and FISA president Jean-Marie Balestre; to his left France's President Mitterrand and the hapless Ayrton Senna, who finished a distant third in his McLaren-Honda. Mitterrand had started his political career as a provincial deputy from this region of central France and his finance minister, Pierre Bérégovoy, had once been the mayor of nearby Nevers. They both supported the construction of this brand-new, state-of-the-art F1 track.

ABOVE British race fans made their annual pilgrimage to Silverstone in the 1980s and early 1990s, banking on Nigel Mansell to give them something to celebrate. At the end of the 1991 British Grand Prix they could hardly have been more delighted. Here he takes his Williams-Renault FW14 past the chequered flag to win his home Grand Prix for the third time – fourth, if you count the 1985 European GP at Brands Hatch as well – after a performance that left all his rivals in the shade. He qualified on pole, but got slightly too much wheelspin at the start, allowing Ayrton Senna's McLaren-Honda to accelerate away into an immediate lead. For a brief moment it looked as though the spectators might have a race on their hands, but Mansell flicked off the rev limiter, gave the Williams a great burst of Renault power going down the Hangar Straight and whistled past Senna into the lead. From that point on he was never remotely challenged. INSET On the final lap of the 1991 British Grand Prix, Ayrton Senna's McLaren-Honda had coughed and spluttered to a standstill, out of fuel, with the embarrassing result that he had to park his car at Club Corner and submit himself to hoots of derision from the Mansell supporters in the nearby

crowd. Cruising on his slowing-down lap, Mansell saw his rival and invited him to hop on the side-pod and take a lift back to the pits. Whether Senna saw anything that particularly interested him during this unofficial view into the Williams-Renault's cockpit is not recorded, but he was certainly increasingly concerned about his McLaren-Honda's continued lack of competitiveness. With eight races completed, after Silverstone Senna still led the title points table on 51, but Mansell was now edging into contention on 33 points. Patrese had spun off after colliding with Gerhard Berger's McLaren-Honda on the first corner of the race, a rare error on the part of the Italian driver.

BELOW Riccardo Patrese qualified on pole position for the 1991 Portuguese Grand Prix at Estoril and finished the day by winning the race in impressive style ahead of Ayrton Senna's McLaren-Honda. By any standards it was an action-packed event. The day had started with FISA president Jean-Marie Balestre attempting to clear the starting grid of surplus individuals, making the tactless error of including Suzy Patrese – Riccardo's wife – in the crowd he was trying to remove to the pit lane. Patrese remonstrated firmly and Balestre backed off! Riccardo led from the start, then Mansell went ahead on lap eighteen before a botched pit stop saw an insecurely tightened right rear wheel detach itself from the car as he accelerated back into the race. The replacement was eventually secured, but the stewards judged that the team had infringed the rule that permits working on the cars only on the inner of the three delineated pit lanes. Mansell was blackflagged and disqualified as a result.

RIGHT Nigel Mansell accelerates back down the Hockenheim pit lane after his sole scheduled tyre change at the end of lap eighteen in the forty-five-lap 1991 German Grand Prix. He had qualified on pole position and, apart from briefly relinquishing the lead to Jean Alesi's Ferrari for a couple of laps while he made that stop, dominated the race to finish fifteen seconds ahead of Riccardo Patrese's sister car at the chequered flag. This result brought Mansell to within eight points of Ayrton Senna at the head of the Drivers' World Championship points table and moved Williams one point ahead of McLaren in the Constructors' Championship. Yet, as far as both Mansell and Williams were concerned, this would represent the season's high-water mark in terms of achievement. Senna, McLaren and Honda were set to bounce back and defend their position over the next few races.

In a cloud of gravel, Nigel Mansell's World Championship hopes for 1991 finally come to an end as his Williams-Renault FW14 flies off the road at Suzuka on the eleventh lap of the Japanese Grand Prix. Mansell had been running in third place at the time, chasing the McLaren-Hondas of Gerhard Berger and Ayrton Senna, which had qualified together on the front row of the starting grid. Going into the fast right-hander beyond the pits, Mansell had the Williams dancing on the outer edge of adhesion as he strained to close the gap to Senna's McLaren. Inexorably the car slid wide, away from the apex of the turn, riding over the kerb on the outside of the corner and then plunging into the gravel. Nigel later attributed his departure from the race, at least in part, to a soft brake pedal. Berger won the race from Senna with Patrese third.

Nigel Mansell and Ayrton Senna side-by-side and wheel-to-wheel battling for the lead of the inaugural Spanish Grand Prix to be held at Barcelona's Circuit de Catalunya in 1991. This confrontation between the two rivals came in the aftermath of what Senna had branded Mansell's unacceptably hazardous driving on the opening lap of the Portuguese Grand Prix the previous weekend. This tension and animosity between the two drivers had been heightened by a fractious exchange between them during the pre-race drivers' briefing at Barcelona. Yet it said much for their professionalism that, although they ran dauntingly close at 180 m.p.h., neither ever seriously weaved at the other or did anything overtly hazardous by the standards of the time. Mansell eventually consolidated his advantage at the head of the field to win by nine seconds from Alain Prost's Ferrari and Riccardo Patrese in the second Williams. Senna was fifth, but had now moved sixteen points clear of Mansell at the head of the table.

Four Championships in Six Seasons

Williams was poised on the brink of its most consistently successful era at the start of 1992. The FW14 challenger was upgraded to a more sophisticated 'B' specification with active suspension and power steering. The team also had the services of a full-time test driver in the form of Damon Hill, son of the two-time World Champion Graham. This reflected how much more work had to be undertaken during the course of an F1 development programme than was the case in the past.

The FW14B proved utterly dominant in Mansell's hands, easily carrying him to the 1992 Drivers' Championship. A falling-out with Frank Williams over the terms of his contract for 1993 meant that Mansell quit F1 for the US CART series – which he won in the following year – while the F1 World Championship was won by his successor at Williams, Alain Prost, securing his fourth title.

Prost would retire after his one season with Williams, and Frank finally signed a deal with Ayrton Senna for 1994, having given the brilliant Brazilian star his maiden F1 test outing over ten years earlier. It promised to be a historic partnership, but was ripped asunder when Senna didn't survive a major accident while leading that year's San Marino Grand Prix at Imola. This was probably the biggest tragedy in the Williams team's history, but the Williams-Renault squad bounced back resiliently.

Damon Hill emerged as a first-rate driver in his own right and would win the 1996 World Championship before Indy 500 winner Jacques Villeneuve – another son of a famous racing father – took over to win the 1997 title, finally bringing down the curtain on the team's terrific partnership with Renault.

1992–97

RIGHT Patrick Head summed up the 1991 season by saying, 'It became clear that we were not going to beat McLaren simply by competing with a car that was the equal of theirs. What we have to do is build a more competitive machine and beat them on superior performance.' Which is precisely what the Williams-Renault squad got on and did. The result of the team's technical development programme was the Williams FW14B, seen here in Nigel Mansell's hands at the 1992 Hungarian Grand Prix. This was a refined and further-developed version of the previous year's car, now fitted with a more sophisticated version of the team's electro-hydraulic gear-change mechanism, the initial unreliability of which had cost the team so many points during the first part of 1991. Patrick also gave the green light for the car to be fitted with the new active suspension system that had been evaluated over approximately 7000 miles by the team's dependable test driver Damon Hill. The car was also fitted with traction control and ABS braking.

LEFT Williams aerodynamicist Adrian Newey (left) together with Patrick Head and Frank Williams early in the 1992 season. Adrian, who had learned much about the importance of detailed aerodynamics while working in the US Champcar arena during the mid-1980s, increasingly took over the role of chief designer as the team's engineering department expanded dramatically during this period. The F1 business had now become too diverse and wide ranging for one individual to keep hands-on control of every aspect of the complicated process. In addition to being a big fan of Mansell, Newey found himself increasingly impressed during 1992 by the methodical manner in which Damon Hill conducted the team's test and development programme. 'He never forgot any instruction you might give him regarding settings of the cockpit controls,' said Newey, 'and his feedback was excellent.' It would also turn out to be a great grounding for Hill's professional future.

Mansell qualified on pole for the first race of the season, the South African Grand Prix at the revised Kyalami circuit, and led from start to finish. Almost seven years earlier he'd won this race on the old Kyalami track at the wheel of a Williams-Honda, the second GP win of his career. He's well out of this picture and scooting away in the lead as Riccardo Patrese's second-placed FW14B heads Ayrton Senna in the previous year's McLaren-Honda MP4/6, the defending World Champion's new car not yet being ready. Patrese would run to a comfortable second place behind Mansell, who symbolically stamped his mastery on what was his twenty-second Grand Prix victory by setting the race's fastest lap with just two laps to go before the chequered flag. 'Williams deserve to be first and second,' said Senna. 'I reckon that third place here was about as good as we could get under the circumstances.'

Mansell and a youthful Michael Schumacher, who finished third in his Benetton, congratulate each other on the winner's rostrum after the Mexican Grand Prix, this time the second race on the F1 calendar. For Mansell it was his second straight win of the year; for Schumacher the first podium finish at the start of an F1 career that would eclipse all others in due course. In this second round of the 1992 World Championship Mansell and Patrese delivered another helping of the medicine they had dispensed at Kyalami. The two Williams-Renault drivers shared the front row of the grid, with Mansell on pole, and they ran first and second for the entire sixty-nine-lap distance. Ayrton Senna, who had survived a heavy crash during practice, ran third in his McLaren-Honda before the transmission broke, allowing Schumacher's Benetton B191B through.

Nigel Mansell speeds to victory in the 1992 Spanish Grand Prix, his fourth straight victory of the season. The race took place in torrential rain and on this occasion the symmetry of the Williams-Renault one–two domination was spoiled when Riccardo Patrese spun off the glistening track while holding second place. Senna simply could not compete with the Williams-Renaults on this occasion and had a couple of spins, the second ending his race. Schumacher's Benetton finished second ahead of Jean Alesi's Ferrari and Gerhard Berger's McLaren-Honda. Again Mansell set the fastest lap of the day, as early as lap ten in this sixty-five-lap race. He now had 40 points after four races, and with Patrese second on 18, one ahead of Michael Schumacher, even at this early stage of the year one was bound to wonder if he could be challenged, let alone overhauled.

Even more of the same! Mansell acknowledges the crowd at Imola as he heads for a remarkable fifth straight victory with another maximum points score in the 1992 San Marino Grand Prix. Again, both Williams-Renault drivers were together on the front row – and again Mansell and Patrese ran non-stop to the chequered flag in one–two formation. For those motor racing insiders who are worried about Michael Schumacher's domination in 2002, it's worth recalling perhaps that precisely the same concerns were being voiced at Imola ten years before, following Mansell's fifth consecutive win. It was left for the team manager Peter Windsor to put the matter into sharp perspective. 'I cannot understand people saying it is boring when you see Nigel Mansell winning the way he has been,' said Windsor. 'I am a traditionalist and a purist and believe that F1 is about the pursuit of excellence in all areas.' To Windsor's credit, in his role as a journalist he would be writing precisely the same in 2002 about Ferrari's stranglehold on the F1 winner's circle.

profile

Frank Williams

Frank Williams retains the same passion for Formula One motor racing as he had when he first fielded a Grand Prix car for Piers Courage in 1969. That passion has in no way been dimmed by the road accident in France just prior to the start of the 1986 World Championship season that consigned him to life in a wheelchair. 'Formula One, to me, is a sport which engenders the fiercest of passions in the many individuals who participate in it,' he says. 'This obviously includes racing drivers, but less obviously includes the people who make it all happen from top to bottom, from left to right, and in every team on the grid. It is an inescapable fact that the people involved are there above all because they love what they do and they have chosen not to earn a living from Formula One, but to participate in Formula One, fulfil their ambitions and their dreams, and thereby make a living.'

Born in 1942 amid the industrial surroundings of South Shields, on Tyneside, Frank grew up with a fiercely independent streak. An early enthusiasm for cars and motor racing was fuelled by an intensive programme of hitch-hiking around the country in order to attend the various race meetings. More than anything, Frank wanted to race, to become a member of what he regarded as an elite. After scrimping and saving, in 1961 he eventually managed to acquire an Austin A35 that had once been raced by future World Champion Graham Hill. He subsequently became involved, initially as a mechanic and later as a driver, in Formula 3 racing, then the lowest rung on the ladder to Grand Prix stardom. Despite scoring a minor international race win at Knutsdorp, Sweden, on 28 August 1966 he eventually decided that he had more commercial acumen than driving talent and retired to concentrate on his business – wheeling and dealing in second-hand racing cars.

As a spin-off from this business Frank started to prepare cars for his friend Courage, a member of the famous brewing dynasty. By 1969 they were in F1 together, and Piers finished second in both the Monaco and US Grands Prix driving Frank's dark blue Brabham-Ford in the days when a privateer could compete in F1 and stand a decent chance of making his mark.

The partnership between Frank and Piers held huge F1 promise, but it was brutally torn apart when Courage crashed the Williams de Tomaso on lap twenty-two of the 1970 Dutch Grand Prix. The car erupted into flames and Piers perished in the inferno. Frank was naturally desolate at the loss of his friend. Yet the tragedy proved a turning point for him. He developed a resilience that would be revealed in his determination not to be defeated by his paralysis sixteen years later.

The story of Frank Williams in F1 in the early 1970s is a tale of initiative, imagination and great good fortune; of ducking and diving, operating his business from a telephone box close to Reading speedway track after the line in the factory had been disconnected. 'It's been like a life of vice,' he says with a wolfish grin. 'I've had a taste of it, and never want to let it go. If I'm guilty of that, so are hundreds of others here in the paddock. I consider myself personally very fortunate to be so mentally involved in it, because it's all engrossing, can be deeply satisfying and it is endless.'

Once Williams hit the F1 big time at the end of the 1980s, Frank never relaxed or eased up. Those years of battling against the odds had taught him that success was difficult to achieve, but even more difficult to sustain. His unflinching determination made Williams a hugely popular team within the F1 community. Race fans see it as embodying all the bedrock qualities of a sport that has, of necessity, learned to exist alongside the commercial demands of outside investors who value it as a blue-chip global communications and promotions medium.

Overwhelmingly, Williams are winners, and they want to win more races and World Championships in the future. Yet Frank retains a healthy respect for every one of his colleagues in the pit lane. Having existed for so many seasons at the back of the F1 pack, he understands just how difficult it is to make the crucial performance break-through to start progressing up the grid. 'There are prob-ably very few teams who are *simply* happy to be here,' he insists. 'They're *all* happy to be here, but I think all our rivals have very competitive ambitions indeed. Nobody simply wants to be in this business to make up the num-bers. It is just too difficult to get into Formula One in the first place. Everybody is driven by a burning ambition to succeed.'

The Williams team scored its first Formula One vic-tory in the 1979 British Grand Prix. Thereafter the team won at least one race every season through to 1988, when it could manage only a couple of second places. An engine supply contract with Renault restored those winning ways in 1989, after which races were won through to the end of 1997. Then came the most painful drought in the team's history, with fifty-four races passing between Jacques Villeneuve's victory in the 1997 Luxembourg Grand Prix and Ralf Schumacher's triumph in the 2001 San Marino Grand Prix at Imola. Frank confesses that it was an uneasy period, to say the very least. 'It was very painful and, more importantly, it was very worrying indeed. Very much a case of making a leap for a ferry which is just leaving port and you can see the gap between the ship and the quay widening and widening and leaving you wondering whether you will ever be able to bridge it again. Then, fast-forwarding to the 2001 San Marino Grand Prix – it was a race of major relief to me at least, if not to every-body else in the team, that we'd bridged the gap and could believe that we could do it again.'

Frank has a deep admiration and respect for F1 drivers. And not just the stars who make the headlines throughout the season. 'I can truthfully say today I admire what Michael [Schumacher] does, Kimi [Raikkonen] does, Juan [Pablo Montoya] certainly, Ralf, and all the front runners on the fast end of the grid, when they're right on it and doing one of their better races. I should also add that the humblest driver on the grid, at the back of the field, has got eight hundred horsepower in a six-hundred-kilo machine, with no room to move about in the cockpit. It's marvellous what they do. Anybody in a Grand Prix, especially in the wet, I just think, Wow, this is truly a remarkable feat of human ability.'

Frank also has many great memories of the top drivers who have achieved success in his team's cars: Alan Jones, Carlos Reutemann, Keke Rosberg, Nigel Mansell, Nelson Piquet, Damon Hill, Jacques Villeneuve, Alain Prost and – not least – the unforgettable Ayrton Senna. 'Fond memories without exception,' he says. 'I can remember wonderful races from each of those drivers: aggressive, spirited and winning. 'That said, I am not into the nos-talgia business. What matters is today or tomorrow, although it is important never to forget that one's most treasured asset is the fund of experience you build up in business and life. Especially in business.'

Frank, therefore, unsurprisingly feels a great affinity with his loyal workforce, the group of specialist techni-cians and backroom boys who work away behind the scenes at the WilliamsF1 Grove headquarters, where the spotlight and glamour of F1 attention seldom shine. 'Yes, we have a very committed bunch back at the factory. I think that is proved by the low staff turnover. It all goes back to my first comment. They must earn a living, but I like to think, for most of them, a high percentage of them, it's a double whammy: earning money and getting job satisfaction at the same time.'

Making these people know that their contribution is valued is a priority for their employer. Frank attempts to make visits to the factory floor on a regular basis. 'Not every day, but certainly several times a week. That's not a measure of laziness, of course, I like to think. I usually get in a bit late and sometimes when I go round the fac-tory floor at eight or nine at night a lot of them have gone home. But it is important for me to keep in touch and communicate with all these people.'

Primarily, Frank Williams is proud to have been involved in F1 during an era of spectacular growth, something that nobody involved in the business could have anticipated twenty-five years ago. 'I absolutely could not have imagined the way in which Formula One has developed,' he admits. 'Bernie Ecclestone saw the poten-tial of it long before the rest of the team owners and, as it gradually dawned on us, so Bernie worked hard to make it spectacularly successful. It is a premier sport, perhaps *the* premier global sport.'

Yet, for all his passionate enthusiasm, Frank remains a pragmatist at heart and believes that F1's status and future development cannot be taken for granted. In his view, F1 needs monitoring carefully year on year, with steps taken to strengthen its infrastructure as and when required. 'I hope F1 stays healthy and its popularity grows,' he says. 'But it always needs thought and nurtur-ing. Many of us in Formula One can't give enough time to do that and this could be to our eventual cost. We must certainly guard against this.'

Against that uniquely spectacular backdrop that is the harbour in Monaco at Grand Prix time, Mansell's Williams FW14B storms over the brow on the approach to Casino Square during the 1992 race that saw his run of success interrupted at last. Having qualified on pole, he led until six laps from the end of the gruelling seventy-eight-lap race. Then, suddenly, his car snapped sideways on a corner. In his mind he believed that the Williams had picked up a slow puncture in one of its rear tyres. He radioed that he was coming into the pit lane. Fresh tyres were fitted, but the delay allowed Senna through to a lead he defended to the bitter end, despite Mansell climbing all over him in the closing laps. It was Senna's fifth win at Monaco, equalling the record of success through the streets of the principality achieved by the late Graham Hill, father of Williams test driver Damon.

An utterly exhausted Nigel Mansell slumps on the ground on the start/finish line after the podium ceremony at Monaco, 1992. Drained and preoccupied, he reflected that victory in the most famous race on the Grand Prix calendar had slipped through his fingers, yet at this moment he could hardly have imagined that this was the last time he would race through the streets made famous by so many of the sport's legendary figures. Mansell had resumed the race after his stop 5.1 seconds behind Senna, but had slashed that to 1.9 seconds with only three laps to go. Yet Mansell was too savvy in the ways of racing to have expected Senna to be intimidated into a mistake in the closing moments of this epic chase. The Brazilian made certain his McLaren was occupying every inch of track that Mansell had his eye on at any given second. Nigel would have done exactly the same, given half a chance.

The Williams team seldom applied team orders to their drivers, but at the 1992 French Grand Prix they made a rare exception after the race was red-flagged to a halt after eighteen laps when it started to rain. Up to that point Riccardo Patrese and Nigel Mansell had been embroiled in a wheel-to-wheel battle for the lead, Riccardo having led from the start and defending himself robustly from his team-mate's challenge. Before the restart, Patrick Head made it clear to Patrese that he was free to defend his position, providing he did not jeopardise the overall team effort. In essence, Patrick was advising Riccardo that if the two Williams-Renaults collided, he would be held responsible. At the restart Patrese again took an immediate lead and, although Mansell overtook cleanly midway round the opening lap, Riccardo slipped ahead again to lead soon after. As he came out of the final corner, Patrese pulled over to the left and raised his arm high in the air, indicating that Mansell should come through; under sufferance, perhaps, but as a loyal team player.

Mansell's Williams takes the chequered flag to win the 1992 French Grand Prix at Magny-Cours, finishing over forty seconds ahead of Patrese, who had been cast in a firm supporting role since conceding the lead to Mansell at the end of the first lap after the restart. This was Mansell's twenty-seventh career Grand Prix victory, matching the tally of Jackie Stewart, and Patrese publicly complimented Nigel on that achievement after the race. It was the perfect note on which to start the build-up for the British Grand Prix at Silverstone the following weekend, a race that had become Mansell's personal fiefdom over the previous decade. Mansell went into his home race with 66 points in the World Championship, 32 ahead of Patrese and 40 ahead of Michael Schumacher, who held third place.

Waving to the crowds in the packed Hockenheim grandstands, Nigel Mansell negotiates his slowing-down lap after winning the 1992 German Grand Prix. Again he started from pole position but on this occasion did not lead every lap of the race, and for once it was not quite the straightforward success he had come to expect. He led from the start, but made his scheduled tyre stop a couple of laps earlier than expected as a warning light came on in the cockpit, alerting him to the possibility of a puncture. He dropped to third behind Senna's McLaren and had a dicey moment trying to pass the Brazilian's car before Ayrton waved him through, knowing full well that the Williams had superior performance. In the closing stages of the race he was deeply concerned about a serious vibration from his left front tyre, the tread on which was 'chunking' quite seriously. It might have rattled Nigel's teeth, but that didn't stop him smiling broadly at his eighth win of the season.

Nigel Mansell, Riccardo Patrese and Martin Brundle beam with delight as they share the Silverstone podium after finishing first, second and third in the 1992 British Grand Prix. In qualifying Mansell had stunned onlookers by claiming pole position with a lap 1.9 seconds faster than Patrese and he was never challenged in the race itself. 'This is a circuit on which you have to commit and I am able to do something that I feel is special at Silverstone which, I think, is the most gruelling physical circuit in the world,' he said. As for the critics who hinted that he was hard on his cars, Renault Sport engineer Denis Chevrier was quick to scotch any such suggestion. 'I can vouch that Nigel does not push his engines too far,' said Chevrier. 'What gets me is that his reputation for being hard on cars seems to be solidly anchored in people's minds, even though all the signs point to the contrary. He never wears out his tyres, nor his brake pads, and his fuel consumption is extremely good.'

Mansell's madly enthusiastic fans invaded the track after his 1992 British Grand Prix victory in a spontaneous outburst of enthusiasm for their hero. Williams test driver Damon Hill, who had made his F1 debut in this race at the wheel of an uncompetitive Brabham BT60, witnessed the drama at first hand. 'I was right behind Mansell and thought we're not going to get out of here alive, because the place was just awash, just swarming with people,' he said. 'I nearly ran over six people. They didn't seem to know that there were other cars on the circuit: they just saw Nigel and leaped on to the track. It was all very difficult.' Hill had played a part in Nigel's victory due to the contribution he had made to developing the Williams FW14B. Two years later, at the same circuit, Damon would get his own reward.

ABOVE The start of the crucial 1992 Hungarian Grand Prix with Riccardo Patrese's Williams FW14B leading into the first downhill right-hander and Mansell and Senna wheel-to-wheel right behind him. Patrese dominated the race before spinning out of the lead on lap thirty-eight, which allowed Senna through into the lead, shadowed by Mansell, who knew that second place was good enough to clinch that long-overdue World Championship. Yet it was not destined to be quite as simple as that. With just sixteen laps to go, Mansell dived into the pits for a precautionary tyre change after the telemetry had indicated he might have picked up a slow puncture. He dropped to sixth, but stormed back through to second place at the finish. Nigel had achieved his life's ambition at last.

RIGHT Mansell and Senna on the rostrum at the 1992 Hungarian Grand Prix, the race that saw Nigel clinch his title with a second-place finish behind the Brazilian driver's McLaren-Honda. 'Feels good, doesn't it?' said Senna, who by that time had three World Championships under his belt. 'Well, enjoy it!' Ironically, Senna was now a component within a complex equation that would make it difficult for Mansell to reach a satisfactory deal to remain with the team in 1993. Four weeks after the triumph in Hungary he decided that he had no option but to announce that he would be leaving not only Williams but F1 at the end of the year. In 1993 he would drive for the Newman Haas Indycar team in the US-based CART Championship, partnering veteran campaigner Mario Andretti. 'We knew in the early months of his second period with us that he would retire if he won the championship,' said Frank Williams. 'This could have been a stronger consideration than we originally thought and whatever the reason for Nigel's retirement we are glad he won the championship he richly deserved.'

Patrese drove his final race for the Williams-Renault squad in Adelaide at the end of the 1992 season. Second place in the Drivers' World Championship had yielded him statistically his most successful season ever, yet there had certainly been times when the popular Italian had seemed frustrated at having to operate in Mansell's shadow. On the strength of his 1991 form it had seemed reasonable to expect Riccardo would run Nigel close for the World Championship, yet this proved to be far from the case. Patrese took the decision to sign a contract with the Benetton-Ford team for 1993 before the end of the 1992 season, a deal that would see him line up alongside Michael Schumacher. If he thought Nigel Mansell was a challenging team-mate, he hadn't seen anything yet. At the end of 1993 he would quit F1 for good and get on with the rest of his life without a trace of regret.

ABOVE Mansell, by now changed back into civvies after his Williams FW14B retired with engine failure, hugs Riccardo Patrese after the Italian driver had won the 1992 Japanese Grand Prix at Suzuka. Mansell and Patrese had privately agreed that the Italian driver would win this race, his first victory of the 1992 season. Nigel pulled away in the early stages before slowing abruptly and relinquishing first place to his team-mate. Thereafter Mansell latched on to Patrese's tail, apparently making him work for his money. Patrese, somewhat confused, then picked up the pace. 'He was pushing me hard and if he was really prepared to let me win the race then I think he should have gone a bit slower,' said Riccardo afterwards. 'Even though I realised he was not fighting me, at that particular moment it was difficult to know what he wanted to do.' Ten laps from the end, Mansell retired and the pressure was off.

LEFT The Williams F1 headquarters at Basil Hill Road, Didcot, which would be the team's base until 1996. When the team first moved there in 1984 it was regarded as a state-of-the-art, lavish even, base for an F1 team, particularly when compared with the small factory unit the team had previously operated from a mile or so closer to the centre of the town. Purpose built for the team over the winter of 1983/4, the factory was officially opened on 16 June 1984 by Michael Heseltine, at that time Member of Parliament for South Oxfordshire and Minister of Defence. The ceremony was also attended by the Lord Lieutenant of Oxfordshire. Three weeks after the factory was opened, Keke Rosberg would score the first victory for the newly formed Williams–Honda alliance in the Dallas Grand Prix.

Frank Williams and Damon Hill together with the 1993 Williams-Renault FW15C after the official announcement that the team's thirty-two-year-old test driver would be promoted to the full-time racing team alongside Alain Prost. Hill had impressed everybody with his testing ability and the commitment he'd applied to driving the uncompetitive Brabham BT60B in a handful of races during the previous season. During his spell as test driver he never allowed himself the mistake of believing that this was a process designed to flatter his status. 'I was not being asked to drive the best F1 car in the business for my own personal pleasure,' he recalled. 'Of course, a test session has nothing like the excitement or glamour of a Grand Prix. But I know that I am making my own individual contribution to the progress of the team. Each time a Williams-Renault won, it was my win in a way as well.' Now his promotion ensured he would get the chance to put his own name in the Grand Prix winners' book.

Alain Prost applied a huge amount of brain power to his motor racing and in 1993 the Frenchman arrived in the Williams-Renault squad with three World Championships under his belt. He had taken a sabbatical the previous year after leaving Ferrari under something of a cloud at the end of 1991, but now he was back in the thick of the action and determined to prove himself as competitive as ever. Prost had previously negotiated to join Williams in the summer of 1989, but eventually switched from McLaren to Ferrari. Patrick Head was impressed with the manner in which Prost went about his business. 'He was immensely talented, but one never got the impression with Alain that he lets anger or any of the more direct emotions overpower his intellect,' Patrick said. 'One of the reasons that Mansell was *so* quick at the British Grand Prix was that his adrenalin was pumped up by his emotion. I don't think Alain ever lets himself veer into that area, which is why his winning came across a bit clinically.' Enough to win a fourth World Championship in 1993, of course.

Alain Prost speeds towards victory in the 1993 South African Grand Prix at Kyalami, his debut race for the Williams-Renault squad. After two successful seasons the FW14 chassis sequence was retired from the scene, leaving Prost and Damon Hill to face their rivals with the evolutionary Williams FW15C, which was powered from the start of the year by a brand-new Renault RS5 V10 engine. The original FW15 had been scheduled to debut at the start of 1992, but Williams instead played things safe by ensuring that the dominant FW14B – a development of the 1991 car – was sufficiently reliable to get the job done. New regulations for the 1993 season required some crucial dimensional changes and the FW15C represented the engineering team's definitive interpretation of those requirements. The new Renault RS5 engine proved generally very reliable with only four failures marring an impressive year of achievement.

RIGHT The opening stages of the 1993 South African Grand Prix featured a great three-way battle between Ayrton Senna's McLaren-Cosworth MP4/8, Prost's Williams FW15C and Michael Schumacher's Benetton B192B. Senna led for the first twenty-three laps before Alain mustered a supreme effort and squeezed ahead going into the fast right-hand corner immediately after the pits. Schumacher passed the Brazilian next time round, but Senna regained the position at his routine tyre stop and just squeezed back into the race second ahead of the Benetton driver. While Prost gradually opened up a decisive advantage, Senna fended off Schumacher's challenge until the Benetton driver dived down the inside of the McLaren under braking for a tight corner. The two cars made light contact and Schumacher spun off into retirement.

LEFT Sometimes things just don't go to plan. One can almost feel Alain Prost's sense of dejection as he steps from his Williams-Renault, which is firmly embedded in the gravel trap at a rain-soaked Interlagos after he spun off while leading the Brazilian Grand Prix. A few spots of rain suddenly became a torrential downpour and just as Prost was about to come in to change to wet-weather tyres, a garbled message over his pit-to-car radio caused him to veer away from the pit-lane entrance and set out on another lap. Seconds later, as Alain approached the first corner of the lap, he found himself coming face to face with Christian Fittipaldi's Minardi, which had spun and stalled, right on the racing line. The Williams aquaplaned out of control, clipped the other car and ended its journey with an inelegant pirouette into the gravel.

LEFT A delighted Damon Hill celebrates his hard-won second place in the 1993 Monaco Grand Prix, a great achievement on his first F1 race outing through the streets of the principality. Twelve months before he had failed to qualify despite a game effort in his uncompetitive Brabham BT60B, but this time he started fourth on the grid in his Williams FW15C and eventually finished second despite being hit and spun round by Gerhard Berger's Ferrari as they jockeyed for position in the closing stages. Hill was mindful of Ayrton Senna's achievement in winning an all-time record sixth Monaco Grand Prix, eclipsing the record of Damon's late father Graham. 'It is thirty years since my father's first victory here and I'm sure he would have been the first to congratulate Ayrton on breaking his record,' he said with great dignity. Senna was much moved by the tribute.

BELOW Prost leads Hill in the 1993 French Grand Prix at Magny-Cours, the third successive race at that circuit where the Williams-Renault team utterly dominated proceedings from start to finish. On Prost's home patch, Damon distinguished himself by claiming the first pole position of his F1 career and the Englishman led up to the scheduled tyre stops, at which point Alain just managed to squeeze ahead, winning by 0.3 seconds after seventy-two laps. Such was the Williams team's domination that Michael Schumacher's third-placed Benetton-Ford trailed them by over twenty seconds by the end of the race. Hill left the race brimful of confidence about his prospects for the British Grand Prix the following weekend, just as Nigel Mansell had done in the previous two years.

LEFT A day of dismay for Damon Hill. Having led his home Grand Prix at Silverstone only for his Renault V10 engine to expire, Hill was to experience another helping of frustration in the German Grand Prix at Hockenheim after his car suffered a tyre failure while leading the race with two laps to go. Admittedly Damon's job had been made easier after Prost was penalised with a stop–go penalty for straight-lining the Ostkurve Chicane – a harsh decision, most reasoned, since Alain had been demonstrably attempting to avoid a likely collision at the time.

BELOW The great day arrives. Damon Hill takes the chequered flag to win the 1993 Hungarian Grand Prix at the Hungaroring, his Williams-Renault FW15C having led every lap in this eleventh round of the World Championship staged on the twisting 2.46-mile circuit just outside Budapest. This success assured Hill a unique position in the sport's history as the only second-generation F1 winner, his father Graham having won fourteen Grands Prix during a career that lasted from 1958 to 1975. 'I thought of my dad and what he might have said to me to keep my concentration up,' said Damon after his Hungarian success. 'And if you knew my dad, you would know that just imagining him talking to me was enough to make me concentrate.'

ABOVE World Champions all. Michael Schumacher (left) has just finished second to Damon Hill in the 1993 Belgian Grand Prix at Spa-Francorchamps while Alain Prost has taken third place. After Hill's victory in Hungary, Frank Williams had joked that, now he'd savoured the taste of winning, he might reel off a succession of victories. And Damon did just that, winning both the Belgian and Italian races. His World Championship crown was still three years away at this stage, while Schumacher – who had won just a single F1 race at the time of this photograph – would come to dominate the sport over the next decade. The time would also come when Michael's relationship with Damon was far more strained than when this photograph was taken.

RIGHT The fourth championship clinched. Prost's Williams-Renault FW15C heads for second place in the 1993 Portuguese Grand Prix. Michael Schumacher's Benetton-Ford squeezed ahead of Prost during the tyre stops and thereafter the German driver refused to be ruffled all the way to the second Grand Prix victory of his career. Prost, the great F1 strategist, weighed up all the options and eventually – after a bold attempt to pass his rival a few laps from the finish – settled for second place. It was another good day for Williams with Damon Hill rounding off Prost's achievement with a strong third place, having stalled on the grid prior to the formation lap and being obliged to start from the very back of the pack as a result.

ABOVE An emotional moment on the morning of the 1993 Portuguese Grand Prix at Estoril. Alain Prost sits alongside Frank Williams at a press conference hastily convened to announce that he would be retiring from driving for good after the final race of the present season. This announcement came a couple of days after Ayrton Senna revealed that he would not be staying with McLaren in 1994, and Prost, who'd spent two tense years as the Brazilian's team-mate at McLaren at the end of the previous decade, had no wish to repeat the experience at Williams. Even though Prost had a two-year contract with the team, Frank simply wasn't prepared to let Senna slip through the net again after several attempts to recruit him had been frustrated over the years. 'Inside the team I have been very happy,' said Prost reflectively. 'I had a fantastic relationship with Damon. It's not often that a driver is happy to see his team-mate win, but I have been with him.'

When Ayrton Senna joined the Williams-Renault team at the start of 1994 it seemed as though a new F1 era was about to dawn. There was a certain comfortable symmetry about the new deal. Frank had given Ayrton his first F1 test at Donington Park back in 1983. Two years later the Brazilian had used a Renault engine to power to his first Grand Prix victory in a Lotus 97T. Even Frank was slightly overawed by having Senna aboard at last. 'When he came here I thought, "Gawd, here we are with Ayrton and we've got this major cigarette company who are going to want him to do this, this and that – it's going to be wall-to-wall aggravation from start to finish." I never thought he would agree to their demands. But we kicked it around and he said, "Yep, I'll do that. Part of the deal." And he did it all without a murmur.' One of the few photographs on the wall of Frank's office to this day is a portrait of this great man.

Damon Hill's Williams-Renault FW16 pauses in the pit lane at Interlagos for a tyre change and refuelling during the 1994 Brazilian Grand Prix where the British driver finished second behind Michael Schumacher's Benetton-Ford. Senna had been pushing Schumacher hard for several laps before spinning off shortly before the finish. He blamed nobody but himself, while conceding that the new car still needed further development work before it was a match for the Benetton. New rules introduced at the start of the season banned electronic systems such as active suspension, ABS braking and traction control and the Williams design team had packaged the new FW16 in a manner that would enhance the airflow over the rear of the car in order to claw back some of the grip lost by these regulation changes.

As if his Brazilian Grand Prix disappointment wasn't bad enough, Senna was left fuming when his Williams-Renault was tapped into a spin by Mika Hakkinen's McLaren on the first corner of the Pacific Grand Prix at Japan's Aida circuit – and then T-boned by Nicola Larini's Ferrari. Senna's Williams can be seen parked sideways at the edge of the gravel trap with the Ferrari nose buried into its right-hand flank. Senna had started from pole position, but Schumacher's Benetton had found better grip on the dusty track surface and reached the first corner in front, never thereafter to be headed. Senna sought out Hakkinen and gave him a piece of his mind. 'I won't tell you what he said,' said Mika, 'but it was not complimentary.'

LEFT Ayrton Senna at the wheel of his Williams-Renault FW16 practising at the 1994 San Marino Grand Prix, round three of that season's title chase. 'The World Championship starts at Imola,' Senna had warned his rivals after disappointing performances in the first two races of the year. Much work had been carried out on the new Williams prior to the Imola race: the profile of the car's nose section was changed, the front wings mounted slightly differently and the cockpit surround altered to suit Senna's personal preference. He started the race from pole position, but the field was slowed by the safety car after just a lap following a collision on the startline between J.J. Lehto's Benetton and Pedro Lamy's Lotus. The safety car pulled in at the end of lap five. Rounding the Tamburello left-hander just beyond the pits at the start of his seventh lap, Senna crashed fatally.

LEFT The Williams pit crew signal to Senna that he has taken pole position for the 1994 Pacific Grand Prix. Qualifying was Ayrton's absolute forte. Like as not, he was always able to squeeze a few extra hundredths of a second out of his machinery. At Imola he would start his last, fateful race from the sixty-fifth pole position of a career that had encompassed just 161 Grands Prix. He had the mental capacity to sit strapped in the cockpit of an F1 car, running through every inch of the circuit in his brain before working out where he could pick up a minuscule advantage. He could then accelerate on to the circuit and translate such a theoretical improvement into reality. All the F1 teams for which he drove during a career that spanned just over ten seasons – Toleman, Lotus, McLaren and Williams – he suffused with the strength of his own personality and inspired the workforce to greater heights.

ABOVE Senna ready to go, on pole position, just before the start of the 1994 San Marino Grand Prix. On the left is his race engineer David Brown, on the right Williams team manager Dickie Stanford. Those close to Senna recall just how much he had been shaken by the fatal accident that had befallen the Austrian driver Roland Ratzenberger during the previous day's qualifying session. This had been the first F1 fatality to take place at a Grand Prix meeting for twelve years and came soon after Rubens Barrichello had survived a major practice accident at the wheel of his Jordan. On the starting grid, Senna had seemed strangely relaxed and at peace with himself. The previous evening he'd talked at length with F1 medical consultant Dr Sid Watkins – a close friend – and even briefly given thought to quitting. Yet the racer's instinct that suffused his soul would quickly overwhelm any lingering doubts he may have felt.

ABOVE A poignant moment at Monaco: Frank Williams in the pit lane while the Brazilian flag flies respectfully in honour of the sport's lost leader. Only a fortnight after Senna's death, attending the most glitzy and glamorous race on the calendar was an extremely uncomfortable experience for many members of the Williams squad. Coming to terms with their loss was never going to be easy, but trying to knuckle down to business as usual in such a high-pressure environment was a test of everybody's resolve. The team fielded just a single car for Damon Hill, who was eliminated in a first-corner collision with Mika Hakkinen's McLaren-Peugeot. 'The whole thing is awful, a very sorry situation,' Hill said. 'The sooner we get away from Monaco and back to some semblance of normality, the better it will be.'

RIGHT Just what the doctor ordered. Damon Hill on the rostrum at Barcelona's Circuit de Catalunya after winning the 1994 Spanish Grand Prix, the next race on the calendar after Monaco. Hill drove well on a day when Schumacher's Benetton became jammed in fifth gear late in the race and the German driver had to settle for second place. Hill and Williams had benefited from a slice of good fortune, but it was precisely the psychological boost they needed. 'This is better than any of my wins last year,' said Hill after the race. 'It made everybody feel better.' The same race saw David Coulthard – the Williams team's test driver – make his Grand Prix debut in the second FW16.

ABOVE Before the start of the Monaco Grand Prix the drivers all lined up to pay tribute to Senna with a Brazilian flag painted on the track where pole position was sited.
The expressions on the faces of the drivers said it all. There was a palpable *frisson* of tension in the pit lane, heightened by the fact that Sauber driver Karl Wendlinger was in hospital, unconscious after crashing heavily into a barrier during practice. It was a peculiar experience to be at Monaco that year. Formula One has a remarkable resilience, the ability to bounce back from all manner of setbacks. But Ayrton's death – and the events that followed it – left the sport winded. 'Everybody in the company was truly shattered by what happened,' recalled Frank Williams. 'At the end of the day the fact is that Ayrton died in a Williams car and that's an enormously important responsibility.'

David Coulthard was a fresh-faced twenty-three-year-old when he was invited to drive the second Williams-Renault FW16 in the 1994 Spanish Grand Prix. He had finished runner-up to Rubens Barrichello in the 1991 British F3 Championship and contested the International Formula 3000 Championship the following year. David hailed from Twynholm, a village near Kircudbright in the Scottish Borders. He was encouraged in his early career by his father Duncan, a successful haulage contractor, and also benefited from the tutelage of Jackie Stewart when he drove for Paul Stewart Racing during his formative years in the junior ranks. At Barcelona, Coulthard qualified ninth and ran an impressive sixth in the opening stages. An electronic glitch with the car's semi-automatic transmission caused his retirement later in the race, but it had certainly been a promising F1 debut for the Scot.

LEFT After Senna's death, Renault – backed by F1 commercial rights holder Bernie Ecclestone – pressed for Nigel Mansell's return to the Williams team, believing that it needed a star driver of proven, front-line calibre to sustain its World Championship challenge. Mansell's 1993 sabbatical in the US Indycar series had been a huge success and he won the CART title at his first attempt. The 1994 season was proving less fruitful and Nigel seemed to be restless. Certainly he was receptive to a deal that would see him drive as many non-clashing F1 races as was possible to fit into his CART schedule. Frank Williams was sanguine about Renault's request to sign Mansell. Since the French car company was largely bankrolling the exercise, he acquiesced to the deal. One thing you could be sure of, Mansell was great box office. The race fans loved him and the media – seen crowding him here at Magny-Cours prior to his comeback drive in the French Grand Prix – simply couldn't get enough of him.

ABOVE Mansell, dressed for his F1 return, chats to Alain Prost in the pit garage at Magny-Cours before sampling a Grand Prix car after an absence of eighteen months. It was clearly going to be fascinating to see how Mansell would shape up. One man who was certainly confident was Damon Hill. 'I view this as an opportunity,' he said. 'I've had a fantastic opportunity to race alongside Alain, Ayrton and now Nigel as well, so that really completes the top three guys of the last ten years. If he beats me, then it shows that I haven't done a good enough job and I'll have to do a better one if I'm going to stay in F1.' In fact, Damon did superbly, outqualifying Mansell to take pole position. He finished second to Schumacher, while Mansell retired with hydraulic failure. It's probably fair to say that Frank Williams and Patrick Head never really expected to come across Nigel Mansell again in a professional capacity after he left their team at the end of 1992. Moreover, signing Mansell to drive a restricted programme of races in 1994 was not straightforward as the British driver shrewdly attempted to negotiate a deal for 1995 on the back of these individual race contracts. Patrick, in particular, did not wish to commit beyond the end of 1994, but Mansell remained a possible candidate for 1995 until late in the year. The team really wanted to bring on Coulthard – which, in the end, they did – while at the same time not wishing to demotivate Mansell in any way while he drove in both the Japanese and Australian races at the end of the season. 'If we take him next year,' said Frank thoughtfully, 'I know what's going to happen. It will be wall-to-wall aggravation between him and Damon.' As it transpired, the partnership was never put to the test.

Silverstone spirit. The patriotic crowd at the 1994 British Grand Prix were again behind Damon Hill, just as they'd supported Mansell before him. And now they had David Coulthard to cheer as an added bonus. Here the Williams-Renault FW16s of Damon and David run in formation in the closing stages of the race, although while Hill is leading, Coulthard is back in fifth place and being lapped by his colleague. Damon had again qualified superbly on pole position and was running second behind Schumacher's Benetton when the German driver became embroiled in a controversy that eventually saw him black flagged and excluded from the race. Hill had yet to beat the Benetton team leader fair and square, but would gradually build the momentum of a title challenge during the second half of the season.

ABOVE The cockpits of the Williams-Renault FW16s of David Coulthard and Damon Hill as they line up in the team's pit garage. The most notable feature on immediate display is the manner in which the cockpit sides have been raised over the past two seasons, offering vastly enhanced lateral protection and support to the drivers' heads in the interests of improved safety. These safety modifications were included among a raft of changes to the technical rules in the wake of Ayrton Senna's fatal accident at Imola the previous year.

LEFT Hill accompanied by Diana, Princess of Wales, on the rostrum after scoring an emotional victory in the 1994 British Grand Prix. It was a great personal success for Hill as this was one race his father Graham had never managed to win, despite leading on several occasions. 'I feel that everything in my life has come together to this point,' said Damon after the race. 'If you believe in destiny, then I honestly believe I was destined to win this race. I had a lot of motivation this weekend, not least because my father never won this race. I feel that this has completed a little hole in my father's record.'

Damon Hill crosses the flag in the 1994 Italian Grand Prix at Monza. Despite this success, Hill was still eleven points behind Schumacher in the Drivers' World Championship table. But with the Benetton team leader serving out a two-race suspension – at Monza and for the forthcoming Portuguese GP at Estoril – now was the moment for Damon to make hay while the sun shone. Hill would win at Estoril, narrowing the gap to a single point. Then Michael beat him into second place in the European Grand Prix at Jerez – before Damon returned the favour by reversing those positions in a rain-soaked Japanese race. They went into the final round with Schumacher one point ahead.

A moment of high drama, captured here by an amateur photographer in the crowd, as Michael Schumacher's Benetton-Ford vaults over the left front wheel of Damon Hill's Williams-Renault during their battle for the lead of the 1994 Australian Grand Prix at Adelaide. Schumacher had run wide out of the previous corner and brushed the wall, but Hill was sufficiently far back not to have witnessed the episode. Damon went for the gap and the two cars collided. The Williams limped back to the pits, but there was no way of repairing its damaged suspension. Race fans would debate for years whether this was a deliberate ploy by Schumacher or just one of those inevitable incidents that are all part of the ebb and flow of racing fortune.

The 1995 F1 season was unique for Williams in that this would be the only year in its history when it raced with an all-British driver line-up. The new Williams-Renault FW17 was unveiled at the team's Didcot headquarters on 21 February 1995. From left to right are pictured Damon Hill, chief designer Adrian Newey, technical director Patrick Head, test driver Jean-Christope Boullion, sponsor representatives and David Coulthard. By the Williams team's exacting standards, this would unfold as an acutely disappointing season, particularly as the FW17 was the fastest car on the circuit. Hill and Coulthard frequently failed to get the best out of their equipment, but in fairness that was only part of the story. Williams also suffered an unusually high level of mechanical unreliability that cost them a string of top-six finishes during the course of the year. The team would end the season with five Grand Prix victories, but key rivals Benetton scored eleven wins.

Damon Hill's Williams FW17 speeds to victory in the 1995 San Marino Grand Prix at Imola as Michael Schumacher's badly damaged Benetton B195 is craned away from the edge of the circuit. The track was wet at the start, but drying steadily, and Schumacher made an early stop to change to slick tyres. He crashed immediately after resuming the race, briefly handing the lead to Gerhard Berger's Ferrari before Hill went ahead on lap twenty-two of the sixty-three-lap race. Coulthard finished fourth on this occasion, so with three of the season's races complete, Hill held a six-point lead over Schumacher and Jean Alesi at the head of the Drivers' Championship table with Williams and Ferrari equal at the top of the Constructors' Championship. Disappointingly, it wasn't destined to last.

Rival team principals Frank Williams and Benetton's Flavio Briatore were thrown together at the centre of a controversy after Michael Schumacher and David Coulthard finished first and second in the 1995 Brazilian Grand Prix. Just prior to the start of the race officials from the FIA revealed to them that there was a discrepancy between the sample of Elf fuel – used by both teams' Renault engines – that had been lodged with the governing body prior to the race and a sample taken at the circuit. After assurances that there was no question of disqualifying the cars until the fuel samples had been returned to Europe for post-race analysis, Williams and Benetton allowed their cars to run. However, a post-race check confirmed the discrepancy with the result that Schumacher and Coulthard were disqualified. The teams appealed, but the appeal was rejected. However, the drivers were permitted to retain their championship points, even though the constructors' points for Benetton and Williams were disallowed.

LEFT David Coulthard abandons the cockpit after his Williams FW17 succumbs to a hydraulic failure during the Spanish Grand Prix at Barcelona's Circuit de Catalunya. It was just one of a series of unfortunate results for the Scottish driver whose first full season in Formula One was blighted not only by too many driving errors but by the lingering effects of tonsillitis that were not fully resolved until he went into hospital for an operation immediately after the Canadian Grand Prix. In Spain Hill also had a disappointing day, dropping from second to fourth on the final lap after the engine cut out due to a hydraulic problem two corners from the chequered flag. This allowed Michael Schumacher to take a World Championship points lead he would never relinquish throughout the season.

RIGHT Damon Hill (right) on the rostrum after finishing second in the Monaco Grand Prix, his failure to win through the streets of the principality proving a psychological body-blow that effectively defined the rest of the season. Michael Schumacher (centre) had won this key race for the second straight year with Gerhard Berger finishing third in the spare Ferrari. Hill had started from pole position and taken an immediate lead, but was never able to pull away decisively from the pursuing Benetton. What made it worse was the gradual realisation that, while Damon was on a two-stop strategy, Schumacher's Benetton was running through to the finish with just a single refuelling stop. That translated into a win by thirty-five seconds for the reigning World Champion and put him five points ahead of Hill in the title race.

LEFT David Coulthard's Williams FW17 spins at the first corner of the 1995 Monaco Grand Prix, pitched into trouble by Jean Alesi's Ferrari, which in turn nudged the Williams into the other Ferrari driven by Gerhard Berger. Funnelling into the tight Ste Devote Chicane immediately after the start, Alesi had tried to make it three abreast on a section of the circuit where two abreast is scarcely feasible, with inevitable consequences for all concerned. The two Ferraris are facing Coulthard in this shot just before the race was red flagged due to the track being completely blocked by the incident. Coulthard would take the spare FW17 for the restart only to retire while running third with a gearbox problem at the end of lap seventeen. The race would be led initially by team-mate Damon Hill, but Michael Schumacher eventually emerged to win and strengthen his grip on a second World Championship title.

Williams expanded its racing into the closely contested British Touring Car Championship in 1995, using Renault Lagunas provided by its F1 engine partner. Here at Silverstone the entire driving team from the Didcot competition operation poses for the cameras with (left) Damon Hill and David Coulthard alongside their Williams FW17 while Alain Menu and Will Hoy accompany their touring car entry. Patrick Head would later compare the atmosphere and modus operandi of Williams Touring Car Engineering to the F1 operation in the years just after he joined in the late 1970s. WTCE in partnership with Renault benefited from all the lessons learned making the F1 operation so successful, with some key personnel making the switch from the Grand Prix team to enhance the touring car challenge. Success came almost immediately with the Williams-Renault Lagunas posting ten race wins in 1995 and clinching the BTCC Manufacturers' Championship at their first attempt.

A disastrous moment in the 1995 British Grand Prix as Damon Hill's Williams FW17 collides with Michael Schumacher's Benetton as the two men battle for the lead with just fifteen of the race's sixty-one laps left to go. The incident provoked a massive furore, although it left both drivers with no more than red faces as they picked their way out of the gravel trap and walked back, separately of course, to their respective pit-lane garages. Needless to say, neither driver believed the incident was his responsibility. Michael thought Hill's lunge down the inside was 'a crazy move' while Damon dismissed it as nothing more than a racing accident. 'I thought I saw an opportunity that I could take advantage of,' said Hill, 'but I am afraid Michael is a harder driver to pass than that – and we had an accident.'

Formula One racing can be a psychologically precarious business for its front-running participants and any momentary deterioration of a leading driver's form inevitably attracts critical scrutiny. In that respect, the 1995 German Grand Prix at Hockenheim could hardly have been a more embarrassing or unfortunate experience for Damon Hill. He started his Williams FW17 from pole position and led over the line at the end of the opening lap. Then, unaccountably, he lost control of his car going into the first right-hander after the pits and spun into the tyre barriers. Here his Williams, wheels locked, is seen broadside across the track as it snaps out of line a few lengths ahead of a disbelieving Michael Schumacher, who was thus handed an easy victory. After pouring scorn on Hill's efforts at Silverstone, Schumacher added to Damon's misery. 'For sure he made a big mistake,' said Michael. 'I saw him go suddenly sideways and thought, "I can't believe this." Then I saw him hit the wall and I thought, "Fine, that's it."'

Track marshals try to restrain Michael Schumacher as he remonstrates with Damon Hill after their second collision of the season in the Italian Grand Prix, another incident that the Benetton driver laid squarely at Hill's door. As if their collision at the British Grand Prix hadn't aggravated their rivalry sufficiently for one season, Hill's Williams FW17 rammed Schumacher off the road at Monza as they were battling for second place behind Gerhard Berger's Ferrari. The two Renault-engined cars were lapping the slow Footwork driven by Japanese novice Taki Inoue as they sped round the fast right-hand Curva Grande and into the braking area for the second chicane. Inoue had hugged the inside line on this corner, forcing Schumacher to lead Hill round the outside. Hill left his braking dramatically late and suddenly found himself spearing into the back of Schumacher's car. Benetton later claimed their telemetry showed that Damon's car was travelling almost 10 m.p.h. faster than their own when the crash occurred, although this was never independently corroborated.

Set against the backdrop of a dramatic sky shrouding the pine forests, David Coulthard leads the Belgian Grand Prix at Spa-Francorchamps, a race that saw him gradually inching away from team-mate Damon Hill. Unfortunately David succumbed to another technical problem when the gearbox began to overheat, resulting in his retirement midway round his fifteenth lap. He later explained that he had seen some oil coming from the rear of his Williams about eight laps earlier, but while that subsequently cleared up, he was worried that the transmission might have leaked away most of its lubricant. A subsequent detailed analysis of the events leading up to the failure revealed that Coulthard had been tapped from behind by Eddie Irvine's Jordan-Peugeot in the first lap scramble round the La Source Hairpin and this had fractured an oil line to the FW17's gearbox.

A happier moment in the season-long rivalry between the Williams and Benetton teams as Michael Schumacher offers a hand of congratulation to David Coulthard following the Scot's maiden F1 victory in the Portuguese Grand Prix at Estoril. Coulthard qualified ahead of team-mate Damon Hill to take pole position and led all but five of the race's seventy-one laps to beat Schumacher by just over seven seconds. Using the revised B-version of the Williams FW17, it was a great result for Coulthard after several near misses during the course of the season, although by this stage in the year it had been confirmed that he was switching to the rival McLaren squad for the following season and his place at Williams would be taken by Jacques Villeneuve. 'In many ways it is difficult to leave Williams after two and a half years,' said Coulthard. Privately he was resigned to leaving the team after Frank and Patrick's reluctance to renew his contract following his failure to match Schumacher's Benetton during their battle for the lead of the German Grand Prix at Hockenheim.

On an unpredictably slippery track surface, David Coulthard's penultimate race as a Williams-Renault driver ended after thirty-nine laps of the Japanese Grand Prix when he spun off the road into the tyre barriers at the high-speed 130-R left-hander just before the pits. It was all part of the learning experience for Coulthard, who would go on to clout the pit wall coming in for a refuelling stop while leading the final race of the season in Australia. He had become a popular and well-liked member of the Williams team and it is possible, had circumstances been different, that he could have emerged as a contender for the World Championship in 1997 had he remained with the team. Frank jokingly remarked about DC: 'I suppose the day will come when I will have to buy him back for a lot more money.' That did not happen, as Coulthard would thereafter drive exclusively for McLaren and, by the end of 2002, had completed six years with the Williams team's main British rival.

Damon Hill on the rostrum at Adelaide after winning the 1995 Australian Grand Prix, a race blighted by so many retirements that the Londoner was two laps ahead of Olivier Panis (left) in the second-place Ligier-Mugen Honda by the time he passed the chequered flag. Gianni Morbidelli (right) took third place in the Footwork-Hart. After his disappointing retirement from the previous race in Japan, Hill cleared off on holiday to Bali with his wife Georgie, thought things over in detail and returned to the final race of the season in a totally revitalised frame of mind. Frank Williams later commented that he was extremely impressed by the way in which Damon had changed. 'Whatever he did, he did it completely on his own,' he added. The 1995 Australian Grand Prix was the last to be held in Adelaide. It was also Hill's fourth win of that season and a success that provided the springboard for a World Championship title bid in 1996.

The new kid on the block: Jacques Villeneuve, seen here demonstrating his ice-skating skills in his native Quebec. He was parachuted into the second Williams-Renault for the 1996 season as successor to David Coulthard. The son of the legendary Ferrari driver Gilles Villeneuve, who was killed practising for the 1982 Belgian Grand Prix, Jacques arrived on the F1 scene in the summer of 1995 when he was invited to test a Williams FW17 at Silverstone. He proved highly competitive from the outset. By then he had victory in that year's Indianapolis 500 under his belt and was poised to clinch the North American-based CART Championship driving a Forsythe Racing Reynard-Ford. Even so, signing this free-spirited Canadian seemed like a risk at a time when memories of Michael Andretti's disastrous 1993 season alongside Ayrton Senna at McLaren loomed large in many memories. Yet Villeneuve struck just the right chord. Willing to learn, yet intimidated by nobody, his preference for baggy overalls and unlaced racing boots gave a misleading impression. He would prove himself a tough racer and was nobody's fool.

Jacques Villeneuve with Damon Hill (centre) and new Ferrari recruit Eddie Irvine on the podium after the Canadian had finished second on his F1 debut in the 1996 Australian Grand Prix. Jacques, who'd celebrated his twenty-fifth birthday on the Saturday of the meeting by placing his Williams FW18 firmly on pole position, very nearly went on to win the race. But a slide over a kerb cracked an oil pipe that left his car trailing a haze of lubricant in its wake. He was told to ease back and conserve the machinery, allowing Hill to win. Villeneuve concealed his disappointment beneath a veneer of self-assurance, knowing full well that he had laid down a marker for the future. He and Hill had also underlined that the Williams FW18, an evolutionary version of the previous year's highly competitive machine, had sustained that performance edge. As events would show, it was also a much more reliable car than its predecessor and the pay-off from that would soon become very obvious.

Damon Hill speeds towards victory in the 1996 Argentinian Grand Prix at Buenos Aires, an apparently seamless performance in which he led throughout. Yet this was a far from straightforward success as Hill was under pressure for most of the race, with Michael Schumacher's Ferrari F310 and the two Benetton-Renaults of Jean Alesi and Gerhard Berger looming large in his mirrors for much of the afternoon. In addition, Damon was suffering from an upset stomach; and an inoperative radio meant that he could not hear any instructions from his pit crew, even though they could hear him clearly. It was Hill's sixteenth Grand Prix win, matching Stirling Moss's career total, and he finished twelve seconds ahead of team-mate Jacques Villeneuve at the chequered flag. With three races completed, Damon had scored the maximum possible and headed Villeneuve by eighteen points in the Drivers' Championship stakes.

Jacques Villeneuve poses for a photo shoot at the 1996 Monaco Grand Prix, an example of one of the many off-track obligations F1's commercial and media-driven dimension increasingly imposes on a driver in this high-visibility sport. The manner in which drivers respond to these commitments offers a fascinating insight into their characters. Some are infinitely obliging and tolerant, appreciating that such events are part and parcel of the celebrity status and earning power that goes with the privilege of being a Formula One driver. Others can be fretful and impatient, feeling perhaps that such episodes are an unwelcome intrusion into their private, off-track life and therefore should be strictly rationed. Some can even be openly hostile and disdainful. In general terms, however, the greater the driver the more balanced and mature is the attitude. For his part, Villeneuve steered a middle path.

Damon Hill heading for his sixth win of the 1996 season in the French Grand Prix at Magny-Cours. Hill had been beaten to pole position by Michael Schumacher's Ferrari F310 and it promised to be a close-fought contest between these two protagonists. Disappointingly for the paying spectators, the battle was neutered before it had started when Schumacher's Ferrari suffered an engine failure and was parked by the side of the circuit on the formation lap. That made things easy for Damon, apart from the fact that the expiring Ferrari had sprayed oil all over his helmet visor, which made life interesting for the first few laps. Hill finished eight seconds ahead of Jacques Villeneuve in another commanding Williams one–two. The Canadian driver displayed great resilience and determination after crashing heavily at 135 m.p.h. during the Saturday qualifying session and having to race wearing a surgical neck support as a result.

Hand-in-hand with the rising international profile of Formula One during the 1990s went the emergence of the celebrity guest syndrome, whereby public figures would be happy to attend Grands Prix and be photographed showing an interest or simply mingling with the paddock glitterati. Here Britain's future Prime Minister Tony Blair, and his wife Cherie, pose for a photo call alongside a Williams FW18 during the 1996 British Grand Prix at Silverstone. The following year, of course, Blair would win the general election, propelling Labour to power. All the signs were that the Blairs thoroughly enjoyed their brief visit to the high-octane world of Formula One.

For the second successive year, Damon Hill's British Grand Prix ended in disappointment, although his 1996 retirement was not down to a driving error or a collision. He'd qualified on pole position in front of an army of his fans, but made a poor start to complete the opening lap in fifth place. He was up to third by lap seventeen and poised to make his first refuelling stop when the Williams FW18 snapped out of his control under braking for Copse Corner, the fast right-hander immediately beyond the Silverstone pits. The problem was eventually traced to a loose front wheel-securing nut, although Damon had suspected that something was going wrong for two or three laps before his retirement. Over the radio link he reported that there seemed to be a strange sensation from the front of the car, almost as if the front anti-roll bar had seized up. Either way, on his latest visit to Silverstone the gravel trap proved to be Hill's final resting place.

The delighted Williams pit crew crowds the Silverstone pit rail yet again to welcome home Jacques Villeneuve as he scores the team's ninth victory in its home round of the World Championship. Seventeen years had passed since Clay Regazzoni's memorable maiden victory in the 1979 race, but the team's passion and thirst for continued success remained undimmed. The home fans may have been deprived of a win from their personal favourite, but Jacques had driven superbly all afternoon, not making a single slip as he underscored the strength of his emerging World Championship challenge. Hill had 63 points, but Villeneuve was now on 48 in second place and intent on maintaining as much pressure as he could over what remained of the season.

Jacques Villeneuve's 1996 World Championship ambitions ended with his Williams FW18 beached in the gravel trap at Suzuka after it had shed its right rear wheel and slithered off the road. Villeneuve had squandered his pole position, dropping to sixth at the end of the opening lap as Damon Hill led. All in all, Jacques had done a great job during his first year as a Williams driver, integrating quickly and smoothly into the team's infrastructure, where he struck up a particularly close relationship with his engineer Jock Clear. If there were any worries about his performances during the season, his preference for a very stiff chassis set-up on the FW18 raised concern about tyre wear, but Jacques seemed happiest with the feel of the car in this configuration. By the end of the season he'd got the legs of Hill, although by then the championship was destined for Damon. Much was expected from Villeneuve in 1997. With good reason.

Jacques Villeneuve subjected Damon Hill's World Championship hopes to a further assault by beating the British driver into second place at the Hungarian Grand Prix, a race effectively decided in the Canadian driver's favour when he completed the first lap in second place and Hill was fourth, losing a second a lap behind Jean Alesi's Benetton during the opening phase of the race. In the closing stages of what was a tactically demanding and complex battle, Hill emerged from his third refuelling stop just seven seconds behind Villeneuve and trimmed that deficit to under a second at the chequered flag. It had certainly been a fortnight of fluctuating fortunes for Hill as he'd been presented with a lucky win in the German Grand Prix two weeks earlier after Gerhard Berger's Benetton-Renault expired while leading a couple of laps from the finish. But there was no such solace to be found at the Hungaroring, where Villeneuve simply out-drove his team-mate and rival.

Damon Hill walks back to the pits after retiring his Williams-Renault FW18 from the lead of the Italian Grand Prix at Monza. He'd been in command at the head of the field when, starting his sixth lap, he clipped a makeshift barrier at the first chicane, spun and stalled. His only consolation at the end of the day was that Villeneuve had finished the race out of the top six with the result that Damon retained his thirteen-point lead in the World Championship. This disappointing race came only ten days after Frank Williams told Hill's lawyers that he was withdrawing from negotiations over Damon's possible contract for 1997 and confirmed that the British driver was free to look elsewhere for a job. Apart from assuring Hill's management team that the decision to terminate those talks had nothing to do with money, Williams declined to discuss the matter any further. A few weeks later it became clear that Heinz-Harald Frentzen had been signed to drive for Williams alongside Villeneuve in 1997.

Renault Sport's technical director Bernard Dudot in light-hearted mood, making a change to the Renault signage to accommodate the fifth straight Constructors' Championship powered by the French company's V10 engine at the end of 1996. For more than two decades Renault had been at the very heart of F1 technology, first with its state-of-the-art turbocharged engines between 1977 and 1986, and latterly with a succession of cutting-edge, naturally aspirated V10 engines that began racing in 1989. Williams and Renault worked very well together as technical partners and there was always a particularly strong mutual respect between Dudot and Frank Williams and Patrick Head. The Williams management regarded Renault Sport as a serious high-technology company with a clear commitment to F1 success and both parties profited hugely by an association that lasted almost ten years. One glance through the Grand Prix record books from 1989 to 1997 tells you all you need to know about this alliance.

A great day for Damon. An emotional moment as the British driver climbs from his Williams FW18 after winning the 1996 Japanese Grand Prix at Suzuka, a success that clinched his World Championship crown. On the right, Michael Schumacher climbs from his Ferrari F310 after finishing just 1.9 seconds behind in second place after a great chase in the closing stages. It was thirty-four years since Damon's father Graham had won the World Championship – the first of his two – in the final race of the season at East London, South Africa. Schumacher summed up Hill's achievement by saying: 'He has waited a long time for this and never gave up, winning eight races this season, which puts his worth beyond doubt.' It was a generous tribute from Damon's arch-rival. From now on, however, their career paths would diverge dramatically: Michael's to three more championship crowns, Damon's to retirement at the end of 1999.

Damon Hill celebrates with his trophies and the 1996 World Championship-winning Williams FW18 at London's Marble Arch. This post-season publicity stunt gained many column inches, but F1 insiders were always aware that Damon seemed vaguely uncomfortable about such high-profile occasions. It was much more to the style of his late father Graham, who lapped up the media attention. Damon by this stage had committed himself to the Arrows-Yamaha team for 1997, a move that, with the best will in the world, was regarded as speculative at best. One of the shrewdest observations about Hill's personality was made by McLaren boss Ron Dennis: 'He craves recognition. I think his placid character doesn't go with his results. If his character was slightly more vivacious or sparkling, perhaps he would be held in higher esteem.'

profile

The team behind the scenes

Dickie Stanford started at Williams in 1985 and immediately went to work on Nigel Mansell's FW10 during the Englishman's first season with the team. The previous year Williams had switched to using Honda engines, and that helped Dickie when it came to securing a job with the Didcot-based F1 team. 'It was January 1985 and I came straight from the Ralt Formula 2 team,' says Dickie, who had unsuccessfully applied for a job at Williams two years earlier. 'I knew all the Honda people. They were going from two mechanics per car to three, so everything fell into place. We had the new carbon-fibre car, the FW10, and then Honda came out with a major engine upgrade in time for the Canadian Grand Prix. We won in Detroit with Keke [Rosberg] and, later in the year, we introduced a rear suspension modification and won the last three races of the season. So it was an exciting time, because the engine was getting better, the chassis was getting better. Williams was the place to be at the time.'

And it was not only because the cars were performing that Dickie felt he'd made a sound career choice. 'I got on extremely well with Nigel; he was very different to the image that comes over on television. He was very determined, yes, but all in all I would say he was one of my favourite drivers.'

Dickie is a Williams man to the core of his soul. He loves the team spirit and relishes being involved in an organisation with so much commitment. 'The big thing about Williams is the dedication throughout the company to win,' he says. 'You look at the whole season, but everybody is just looking for the next race. Even if you qualify well nobody gets too excited because they're all interested in winning. Nobody remembers who came second. The working environment is very good. Frank and Patrick talk to the workforce and everybody is well informed as to what is going on all the time, what developments there are and so on. You get your chance to ask any question, even though it's in front of three hundred other people. Most of the people within Williams have been racing at some stage or another, so they know the score. You will always get a decision from Frank or Patrick straight away. And there's no "Mr Williams" or "Mr Head". It's "Frank" and "Patrick". If you call Frank "Mr Williams" you get told straight away. This breaks down lots of barriers. It makes Frank Williams accessible to everybody. The cleaner is treated as well as the team manager. Frank knows as much about the cleaner as he knows about me.

'The way the system's run is that they have all their meetings throughout the week, but there are no closed doors in the organisation. If, let's say, Carl [Gaden], the chief mechanic, wants to speak to the drawing office, then they will talk to him. He can have immediate access to Patrick. No problem.'

Being a Williams employee puts you in the F1 and motor-racing elite. 'Everybody thinks it's a great place,' Dickie enthuses. 'When I started there were about sixty people at Williams; now it's over four hundred. But you still know all the key faces. We've had great drivers every year, sometimes we've won a championship, sometimes we haven't. But the commitment has always been there. Most of the drivers come to the factory and make sure they talk to the entire workforce. Montoya has been in the factory more than most drivers; you might find him in the machine shop, just chatting with the guys.

'You can relate all the time to Frank and Patrick. Rather

then being just an employee, you are part of the company. There is a collective pride at being part of the Williams family. There are lots of people who've found that out over the years when they've gone off to seek other opportunities. The grass isn't always greener somewhere else.'

Bernie Jones is one of the Williams team's oldest employees. He's set to retire in the spring of 2003 when he reaches his sixty-fifth birthday. Bernie began with the company when the foundations of the current organisation were being laid, the fledgling F1 operation running a private March-Cosworth for the Belgian driver Patrick Neve.

'I started with Frank on 11 July 1977,' says Bernie. 'I started my career in general engineering, then went into the aircraft industry and on to Leyland, working in their experimental department, and then I came here. The original premises on the Didcot industrial estate near the station were pretty small, little more than a lock-up really. It had a machine shop, a little area for sub-assembly and one car packed in. There were about seventeen or eighteen of us at the time and one of the first jobs I had was to build our own chassis jig to start on the FW06 for 1978. We all knew each other, it was a real family affair, if you like. You saw Frank and Patrick every day and they came round and spoke to us all.

'The company has grown now and it's not quite the same as it was. In those early days it was brilliant to work there: a real sense of togetherness, everybody helping each other. Now it's so vast, you obviously don't know half the people. But in the late seventies and eighties Williams was the place to be in the Formula One business. It was a really electrifying atmosphere. Then in 1984 we moved to Basil Hill Road. It was much bigger, but you still met most people every day. It was a really lively place.'

During his career with Williams, Bernie has seen many changes in the manufacturing process, principally the switch from aluminium to carbon-fibre composite chassis technology. 'I came here originally to build the chassis and wings out of aluminium,' he explains. 'I've worked on one

hundred and thirty-three chassis in my time, up to FW19 in 1997. And that's the last time we won the World Championship.'

Bernie hasn't been to many of the races over recent years, despite the fact that Frank makes sure that the workforce can go to Silverstone if they want to. 'Years ago, Frank would give you a ticket for the British Grand Prix and if you didn't show your face in the pits it would be a case of "Where the bloody hell were you?" when you saw him the following Monday. Nowadays you can't even get into the pits!'

Donna Robertson cannot believe how long she has been at Williams. She joined as a receptionist in 1987, the season in which the team and Nelson Piquet won the World Championship. 'I was only here a month as a temp and already I received my first bonus,' she recalls. 'I went away with a few extra bob, bought a time-share in the Lake District and never looked back. I was between jobs when I took the temporary job here and have stayed ever since. I haven't really progressed much, you might say, but I just love it and here I am. I've got an assistant now after fifteen years. When I look back at all the race and test itineraries, none of which I've ever thrown away, I realise just how much work we did then. We didn't struggle, but we did it pretty well on our own and we certainly worked hard.

'I was looking at the personnel numbers, and although the company has grown to around four hundred and fifty now, the race and test team hasn't grown so much. We've always run three cars and there are now sixty-four people who go to the races. It's marketing and electronics that have really grown dramatically over recent years.

'To me, Williams means fun, looking forward to a Grand Prix every two weeks, having people like Frank and Patrick always there. Not too political an environment, still a family – even though it's a big family now – and being able to say what you think without anybody taking it the wrong way. There is also a great interest in motor racing from the top down. And everybody who comes to work here has that passion for the sport.'

Flying high: Jacques Villeneuve skiing in extrovert style during the winter of 1996/7. Some people might be forgiven for thinking this was an unnecessarily hazardous occupation for a professional racing driver, particularly bearing in mind that even a slightly injured limb might mean three or four races sitting on the sidelines. Yet it was typical of Jacques's resolute determination to be his own man that he should confront life exclusively on his own terms, and that meant doing what he wanted to do. This was admirable as far as it went, but even for one of the best drivers in the F1 pit lane it can be a strategy strewn with pitfalls. Jacques would drive superbly for much of the 1997 season, but he had a defiantly independent streak when it came to setting up his cars and this sometimes resulted in differences of opinion between him and the technical staff.

Heinz-Harald Frentzen came to the Williams team at the start of 1997 after three seasons driving for the Sauber F1 team. After Ayrton Senna's death in 1994, Frentzen had been approached and asked if it would be possible to negotiate a release from Sauber to join the beleaguered Williams squad. Heinz-Harald, flattered though he was by all the attention, felt that his first loyalties were to Sauber, who had given him his F1 chance in the first place. Williams continued to monitor his progress over the next three seasons and eventually decided to conclude a two-year deal with him for 1997 and 1998. Yet his relationship with Williams when it came was not destined to be a success. In fact, there were moments during 1997 when one sensed senior personnel within the team stopped just one word short of admitting that signing him had been a dreadful error of judgement. Certainly, it was widely believed that Damon Hill would have achieved more than the gentle and mild-mannered German had he stayed on.

One significant loss from the Williams team's technical armoury in November 1996 was chief designer Adrian Newey, who was unable to agree terms for a new contract. The highly respected F1 engineer spent the next eight months on 'gardening leave' before joining rivals McLaren-Mercedes as technical director in the summer of 1997. Patrick Head would generously give Newey much of the credit for the aerodynamics and general technical layout of the Williams FW19. It was Adrian's experience working for the March Engineering organisation during the mid-1980s on the US Indycar trail that earned him a reputation as an astute aerodynamicist and those skills were later further developed with a spell at the Leyton House F1 squad. Adrian joined Williams in 1990 and played a leading role in developing the 'undercut' nose profile used by the Williams FW14 and on the team's subsequent F1 challengers.

Jacques Villeneuve and Heinz-Harald Frentzen strapped into their Williams FW19s all ready to leave the pit lane at Melbourne prior to the start of the 1997 Australian Grand Prix. The FW19 was yet another logical evolutionary development of the car that had immediately preceded it, fitted with a more compact transverse gearbox and an extensively revised cooling system. Engine partner Renault confirmed at the start of the year that it would be withdrawing its factory support from F1 at the end of the season, but its design team under Bernard Dudot certainly showed no signs of easing up on the development front. For 1997 Renault produced an all-new RS9 V10 engine, featuring a wider 71-degree angle as well as being lower and lighter. From the start of the season it was reputed to develop a highly competitive 740 b.h.p. at around 17,000 r.p.m.

BELOW Carlos Reutemann, one of the Williams team's most distinguished and respected 'old boys', is reunited with his former employer at the 1997 Argentinian Grand Prix. On a weekend when Jacques Villeneuve won the race ahead of Eddie Irvine's Ferrari, Reutemann was as big a celebrity in the paddock as any of the competing drivers. For many years the governor of his country's Santa Fe province, Carlos had frequently been tipped as a likely presidential candidate, although those close to him believed he had too much political savvy to run for such a volatile post that might jeopardise his enormous popularity and respect. Frank always had a great deal of time for Carlos Reutemann, loving his reticent personality and – on his day – a driving genius that was a match for any of his contemporaries.

LEFT Heinz-Harald Frentzen's Williams-Renault FW19 storms past the pits at Melbourne's Albert Park circuit, leading the first race of the 1997 season. In the closing stages of the race he was in second place and whittling down David Coulthard's lead when his car's left front brake disc disintegrated as he slowed for the right-hander beyond the pits, pitching the Williams into a sudden spin that ended in the gravel trap. It had been a disappointing first race of the season for Williams as Villeneuve was bundled into retirement on the first corner after a brush with Eddie Irvine's Ferrari. Yet the fact remained that the Williams FW19 was probably still the best car on the circuit, even allowing for the fact that McLaren and Ferrari were both dramatically strengthening their challenges.

Heinz-Harald Frentzen and his girlfriend Tanya – later his wife – celebrate with the winner's trophy after his victory in the 1997 San Marino Grand Prix at Imola. Frentzen's success made it three wins for the Williams-Renault squad out of the first four races of the season. He won by over a second from his old rival Michael Schumacher's Ferrari F310B and, amazingly, it was Heinz-Harald's first race win for almost four years. His last victory had been a round of the Japanese Formula 3000 Championship in 1993 and, after seemingly losing his way during at least two of his first three races for Williams, it seemed as though the Imola success had confirmed his status as a regular front runner. 'This is like oil on my soul,' said Frentzen emotionally. Sadly, it wasn't to last.

A rear shot of Jacques Villeneuve's Williams-Renault FW19 heading for the team's hundredth F1 victory, appropriately enough in the British Grand Prix at Silverstone. The Canadian achieved this landmark success after what had seen a struggle against the odds that was only resolved in his favour with a slice of good fortune in the closing stages. Michael Schumacher's Ferrari F310B retired from the lead with a wheel-bearing failure, while Mika Hakkinen's McLaren-Mercedes succumbed to engine failure only six laps from the chequered flag, handing the Williams driver another win. Note the enigmatic 'R.?' identification on the rear wing at this race where tobacco advertising was not permitted and the customary Rothmans branding could not be displayed.

OVERLEAF The Williams squad follows its customary well-drilled technique to service Frentzen's car at a routine refuelling stop during the 1997 Spanish Grand Prix at Barcelona. Frentzen could only finish eighth on this occasion after a poor start from second place on the grid. Tyre wear was a problem for many competitors on this day and Heinz-Harald, who came to Williams with a reputation as being easy on his rubber, admitted the whole affair had proved to be a bitter disappointment. He explained that he'd been unable to push hard throughout the race as his rear tyres had proved unexpectedly prone to blistering after a generally trouble-free practice and qualifying. What made it worse for Frentzen was that Jacques Villeneuve had sailed to another impressive victory, edging back into a three-point championship lead ahead of Michael Schumacher.

BELOW Some days things just don't go to plan and it's on those occasions when it is important for a Formula One pit crew to keep its cool. Early in the British Grand Prix a problem with the front left wheel working loose caused Jacques Villeneuve to suspect that the Williams FW19's power steering had developed a fault. When he brought the car in for his first refuelling stop it was stationary for 33.1 seconds, usually enough of a delay to write off any competitor's chances. In the closing stages of the race he was boxed in behind Mika Hakkinen's McLaren, but reckoned he had sufficient tricks up his sleeve to outwit the Finn over the last few laps. As it was, Jacques didn't need to use his planned *banzai* manoeuvre as the McLaren's engine expired. The real racer in him had been thwarted!

The defining moment of the European Grand Prix when Michael Schumacher deliberately steers his Ferrari into the left-hand side-pod of Jacques Villeneuve's Williams FW19 as the Canadian driver makes a legitimate passing move with twenty-one laps left to run in this World Championship decider. Schumacher came off worse after this incident, his Ferrari skidding to a halt in the gravel trap, out of the race. Villeneuve was worried that his Williams might have suffered serious damage in the collision and eased back to finish third behind the McLaren-Mercedes team of Mika Hakkinen and David Coulthard. So Villeneuve earned four points, enough to put him three clear of Schumacher in the Drivers' Championship. By clinching the crown, Jacques achieved something his illustrious father had never quite managed during his career with Ferrari.

The start of the crucial final race of the 1997 season saw the two Williams-Renaults of Frentzen and Villeneuve elbowed aside as they jostled into the first corner of the European Grand Prix at Spain's Jerez circuit. Schumacher started the race leading the championship by one point from Villeneuve. From the outset this proved to be an overtly tactical race conducted in a crackling atmosphere of tension and expectancy. Schumacher and Villeneuve raced through their first routine refuelling stops to re-emerge at the head of the field, just 0.9 seconds apart after thirty laps of the race, with the German in the lead. Villeneuve seemed to need a miracle to deny the Ferrari ace.

CHAPTER FIVE

Winners Again

After achieving two back-to-back World Championships the WilliamsF1 squad faced lean times in 1998, buying its engines from Mecachrome, a Renault-affiliated company. Jacques Villeneuve and Heinz-Harald Frentzen continued as the team's drivers, but access to the F1's winner's rostrum was fast becoming reserved for Ferrari's Michael Schumacher and McLaren's Mika Hakkinen and David Coulthard.

This trend continued into 1999, when WilliamsF1 switched both of its drivers – a rare decision historically – to recruit Ralf Schumacher (Michael's younger brother) and the CART star Alex Zanardi. Again, Ferrari and McLaren remained the prime targets to beat, but while Ralf Schumacher began to develop the potential he had shown during his two seasons with Jordan, Zanardi simply couldn't get to grips with contemporary F1 and left the team at the end of the season.

In 2000 the team's new partnership with BMW commenced and the twenty-year-old British rising star Jenson Button joined Ralf Schumacher in the team. By now Ferrari was getting the upper hand over McLaren, but the WilliamsF1 BMWs made steady progress in their first season.

In 2001 Juan Pablo Montoya, former CART Champion and Indianapolis 500 winner, replaced Button alongside Schumacher and the team finished third in the Constructors' World Championship in its first season on Michelin rubber.

The next year Ralf Schumacher scored the team's sole victory in the Malaysian Grand Prix, but Montoya continued to emphasise his raw speed with seven pole positions, and the team moved up to second place in the Constructors' Championship. Beating Ferrari was now the overwhelming priority as the 2003 season beckoned.

1998–2002

Colombian driver Juan Pablo Montoya (front left) and Brazil's Max Wilson. Montoya had first met Frank Williams at the 1997 British Grand Prix, where Villeneuve claimed WilliamsF1's one hundredth Grand Prix victory. He had shone in his first season of Formula 3000 during 1997 and would go on to win the title in storming style during 1998. Montoya clearly had a great future in racing, and although he would not make it into the WilliamsF1 line-up for 1999, he achieved his ambition two years later after a successful spell competing in the USA. After nine years, the engine partnership with Renault Sport that had yielded such spectacular and consistent success had come to an end with the withdrawal of the French company from F1 as a works supplier. Instead the team was left to lease what amounted to 'customer' versions of the Renault V10 from its subsidiary, Mecachrome, on a purely commercial basis. The WilliamsF1 FW20, which now carried the red livery of Rothmans' Winfield brand, was also the team's first car for several years not to have input from Adrian Newey, who had left for McLaren more than a year earlier. Gavin Fisher had taken the role of chief designer, and with aerodynamicist Geoff Willis was responsible for the FW20. This was the first Williams to conform to the narrow-track, grooved-tyre regulations that had been controversially introduced for the start of the 1998 season.

The boys to entertain you. The WilliamsF1 team's complete driver line-up during 1998 included two test drivers, a reflection of just how much development work a top F1 operation needed to undertake to retain its competitive challenge throughout a season. Jacques Villeneuve and Heinz-Harald Frentzen (back row) were assisted by

Heinz-Harald Frentzen opened the 1998 season on an encouraging note by taking his WilliamsF1 FW20 to third place in the Australian Grand Prix at Melbourne, although he was convincingly outpaced by the new McLarens of Mika Hakkinen and David Coulthard, which finished in one–two formation at the head of the pack. The fact that Frentzen was lapped by the two McLarens was also a touch depressing. The German driver had qualified fifth and after the race expressed the view that the gap between the McLarens and the FW20 was probably not as big as it had looked at this event. This was a distinctly overoptimistic conclusion. Jacques Villeneuve, who had qualified fourth, ended the race in sixth place, slowing in the closing stages as he was worried by high engine temperatures caused by blocked radiator intakes. 'I am not used to being a victim,' he said, shrugging philosophically.

Jacques Villeneuve kicks up the dust and debris as he takes his WilliamsF1 FW20 on a spectacular off-track excursion during free practice for the Brazilian Grand Prix at Interlagos. This incident – which the team attributed largely to Jacques's insistence on running a very stiff chassis set-up, which in turn made the car nervous to drive on the bumpier sections of the track and caused it to spin off – resulted in the FW20 chassis being quite badly damaged and Villeneuve had to take the spare car for qualifying. He qualified a distant and disappointing tenth on a day that his team-mate Frentzen managed third on the grid. Heinz-Harald powered to fifth in the race, Jacques to seventh. Both WilliamsF1 drivers ran a two-stop strategy on this occasion. 'The way we were getting through our rear tyres on Friday and Saturday meant that a one-stop run was impossible,' said Jacques.

Both WilliamsF1 FW20s managed to finish on the same lap as David Coulthard's winning McLaren during the San Marino Grand Prix. Heinz-Harald Frentzen took fifth place 22.8 seconds behind team-mate Jacques Villeneuve. The team arrived for this race fresh from what had seemed like a productive test session at Spain's Jerez circuit, but when it came to qualifying a lack of rear-end grip continued to be the abiding problem. 'I think we are both trying to over-drive this car faster than it wants to go,' said Jacques after qualifying sixth on the grid, two places ahead of Frentzen. By the end of the race WilliamsF1 retained third in the Constructors' Championship table, but McLaren and Ferrari were pulling steadily further ahead.

Heinz-Harald Frentzen's WilliamsF1 FW20 is refuelled at a routine pit stop during the Spanish Grand Prix at Barcelona by a mechanic wearing the distinctive yellow overalls of the team's fuel sponsor Petrobras. Frentzen had qualified only thirteenth for this race – three places behind Jacques Villeneuve – and struggled through to eighth at the finish with his colleague ahead of him yet again, this time by two places. In the closing stages of the race Frentzen had perked up considerably, slicing his way through from twelfth to his eventual finishing position with some determined overtaking during the last five laps of the race. Even so, WilliamsF1's season was developing a distinctly disappointing trend, far from what they had been used to over the previous decade.

Movie star Sylvester Stallone chats to Jacques Villeneuve as the Canadian sits strapped in his WilliamsF1 FW20 prior to the start of the Monaco Grand Prix. It is doubtful whether Jacques had time for more than a few fleeting pleasantries with his celebrity guest, for practice and qualifying through the streets of the principality on this occasion had proved a lurid affair. The first free practice session had seen his WilliamsF1 FW20 slide into a barrier after tangling with slow-coach Ricardo Rosset's Tyrrell. On Saturday morning Jacques spun into the barrier at Ste Devote, damaging the car, and then could only qualify thirteenth. Optimistically, he and the team agreed on a one-stop strategy for the race and it worked pretty well, vaulting him up to fifth place at the finish, even if it was more than a lap behind Mika Hakkinen's winning McLaren.

RIGHT A frustrated Heinz-Harald Frentzen abandons his WilliamsF1 FW20 during the Monaco Grand Prix after a collision with Eddie Irvine's Ferrari. The incident happened as early as lap ten of the seventy-eight-lap race when Irvine dived down the inside of the WilliamsF1 driver under braking for the Loews Hairpin and tapped his rival into the guard rail. Irvine shrugged the incident aside as one of those occasional episodes that are part and parcel of the frustrations bred by racing in such a tight environment as Monaco. The Ulsterman could take a philosophical viewpoint, of course, as his Ferrari survived unscathed from the accident to finish third in the race. Frentzen was not so phlegmatic, although he had a long walk back to the pits during which his temper cooled down.

LEFT An absolutely furious Heinz-Harald Frentzen climbs from his WilliamsF1 FW20 after being pushed off the circuit by old rival Michael Schumacher's Ferrari during the Canadian Grand Prix at Montreal. Schumacher had just emerged from the pits after refuelling and apparently did not see Frentzen's third-placed car. He moved to the right and pushed Heinz-Harald straight off the track. 'I am really angry about what he did,' said Frentzen. 'He's the guy who is always complaining about these things.' Schumacher adopted a conciliatory tone. 'If it was my fault, I apologise,' he said, 'but I just didn't see him at all.' Williams later lodged a rare protest against Schumacher, but it was rejected by the stewards. 'I was making a voice heard, rather than seeking redress,' said Frank. 'I felt that Michael's behaviour was out of order on the Grand Prix track, and it's not for the first time.'

Jacques Villeneuve's WilliamsF1 FW20 heads for sixth place in the Austrian Grand Prix at the A1-Ring. Starting from eleventh on the grid, the race had been frustrating for Villeneuve, who'd spent many laps trapped behind Jarno Trulli's Prost-Peugeot. It was at this race that Villeneuve confirmed that he would be leaving WilliamsF1 at the end of the season to pursue his career with the newly formed British American Racing organisation. 'I was happy at Williams,' he admitted, 'although the results just did not come this year as we had wanted them. I expect next year to be an interim season for them and I don't want to do another season like this one.' As it turned out, things would be substantially worse for the Canadian at BAR.

LEFT Heinz-Harald Frentzen overshoots his position as he comes in for a refuelling stop on his way to fifth place in the Hungarian Grand Prix. Frentzen qualified seventh after suffering badly with a stomach bug, vomiting uncontrollably and unable to keep down any food. After finishing the race he was dangerously dehydrated and, on medical advice, flew immediately to Vienna where he spent the next four days recovering. Team-mate Jacques Villeneuve qualified sixth and finished third, his second successive race on the rostrum, which certainly made it one of the better race results in what was turning out to be a consistently disappointing season for the WilliamsF1 squad.

RIGHT Villeneuve strapped in the cockpit of his WilliamsF1 FW20 conferring with his race engineer Jock Clear during the weekend of the Luxembourg Grand Prix at the Nurburgring where the Canadian driver finished a disappointing eighth. During his three years at WilliamsF1, Jacques developed a close professional working relationship with Clear, and it was little surprise when Jock moved to BAR with his driver at the end of the season. By the end of this race weekend it had also become public knowledge that there would be two new drivers in the WilliamsF1 camp for 1999: Ralf Schumacher and CART star Alex Zanardi. Frentzen would be off to join the Jordan squad, and the slightly disappointed WilliamsF1 test driver Juan Pablo Montoya would join Chip Ganassi's CART team in the USA as replacement for Zanardi.

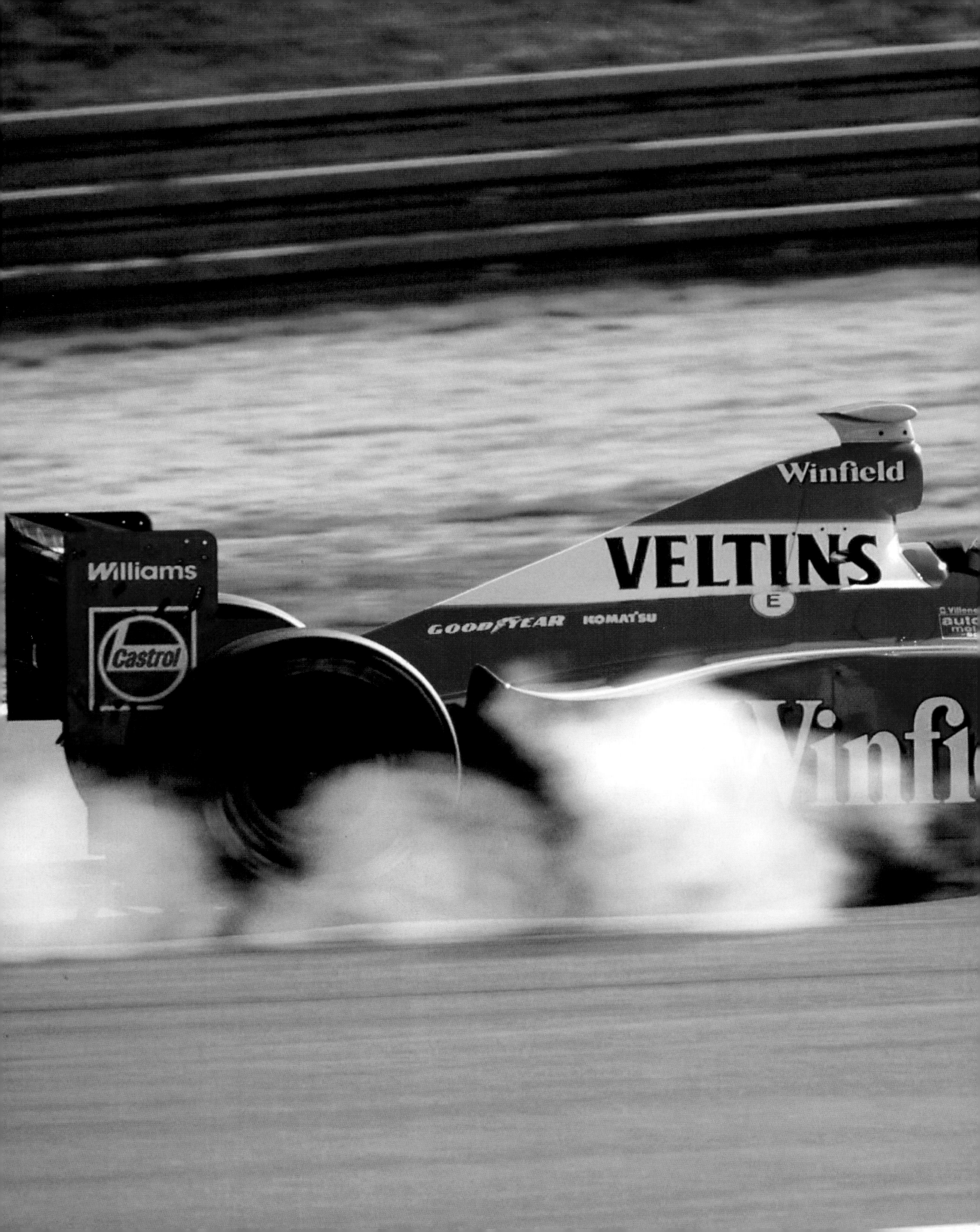
Winfield
VELTINS
E
Williams
Castrol
GOODYEAR
KOMATSU

End of a great partnership: Jacques Villeneuve locks up a front wheel of his WilliamsF1 FW20 at the Nurburgring, two races prior to the Japanese Grand Prix at Suzuka, his swansong for the team that had carried him to the World Championship twelve months earlier. Heinz-Harald Frentzen had looked on course for fourth place at this final race of the year but, having grappled with inoperative power steering for most of the race, was jumped by Damon Hill's Jordan at the very last corner. 'I don't think Heinz could have been watching his mirrors,' commented Patrick Head crisply. WilliamsF1 had finished the year third in the Constructors' Championship on 38 points, almost 100 points behind second-placed Ferrari. It was the first season since 1988 that the team had failed to win at least a single Grand Prix.

LEFT The new team: Ralf Schumacher (left) and Alex Zanardi line up with motorcycle star Mick Doohan to celebrate the start of the new F1 season in Melbourne prior to the 1999 Australian Grand Prix. Ralf came to WilliamsF1 with two years' F1 experience under his belt with the Jordan squad, while Zanardi, who had raced with Lotus back in the early 1990s, had established much of his reputation racing in CART over the subsequent few seasons. Recruiting Zanardi would be a bold gamble which, as it turned out, was fired by misplaced optimism. By contrast, Ralf would be starting out on a journey with WilliamsF1 that would see him develop into a proven front runner and accomplished contender for Grand Prix victories over the next four seasons.

RIGHT Geoff Willis and Gavin Fisher (right) were, respectively, head of aerodynamics and chief designer for the WilliamsF1 team at the start of the 1999 season. The WilliamsF1 FW21 was much lighter than its immediate predecessor the FW20 and had a lower centre of gravity, but it still proved to be a disappointment for a team used to winning races on a regular basis. The car was again powered by what amounted to a customer Renault V10 – now rebranded a Supertec – and the team was running on Bridgestone tyres following the withdrawal of Goodyear from the F1 business at the end of the previous season. By the start of 1999 it had long since become clear to Frank Williams and Patrick Head that it was essential to be in a long-term partnership with a factory engine supplier in order to achieve sustained F1 success. Such a partnership with BMW was already established for 2000, but for the time being WilliamsF1 had to press on with the uncompetitive FW21.

RIGHT Alex Zanardi had a disappointing debut for the team in the Australian Grand Prix, qualifying fifteenth, being forced to take the spare car due to a clutch problem and then crashing heavily after twenty laps. Sadly, it would set the tone for his season. Coming straight from a Champcar, which races on slicks, Zanardi found it difficult to come to terms with the 'edgy' feel of the grooved Bridgestones on the WilliamsF1 FW21. There was also a feeling within the team that perhaps Zanardi was not the fittest of drivers and could have been a little more focused and committed to the business of integrating with the team. That said, everybody agreed that he was a thoroughly nice fellow. Sadly, perhaps, in F1, as in any professional sport, the nice guys are not always the most successful.

The podium at Melbourne with Ralf Schumacher (right) celebrating his first outing as a WilliamsF1 driver with third place behind Ferrari's Eddie Irvine and Heinz-Harald Frentzen, now at Jordan. It was a steady run for Ralf from eighth place on the starting grid, despite his WilliamsF1 FW21 shedding one of its aerodynamic bargeboards in the closing stages of the race. The younger Schumacher certainly finished the day in an upbeat and optimistic frame of mind, reporting that the car was quite well balanced throughout. His first season at WilliamsF1 would see Ralf mature into a rounded and complete performer, both on and off the track. By the end of the year his formidable driving ability was being complemented by a relaxed professionalism away from the cockpit.

ABOVE Ralf Schumacher's WilliamsF1 FW21 retired from the San Marino Grand Prix at Imola when a fire in the airbox burned through the wiring loom of the injectors. He had resumed the race after a refuelling stop in fourth place just before the half-distance mark. This was a particularly disappointing day for the WilliamsF1 team as Alex Zanardi spun off in the closing stages of the race. Yet WilliamsF1 insiders could at least take heart and look forward to 2000 knowing that the Williams-BMW F1 prototype had the previous week undergone its first trials at the Miramas test track, near Marseille. Driven by Jorg Muller, the Munich-built V10 engine had been installed in a WilliamsF1 FW20 chassis for its first promising tests.

RIGHT The 1999 Monaco Grand Prix proved extremely frustrating for the WilliamsF1 team, but at least Alex Zanardi managed to post his first race finish of the season, bringing his FW21 home eighth, two laps behind Michael Schumacher's winning Ferrari. In fairness, on this occasion it was not the driver's lack of aptitude or skill that was to blame. On lap fourteen he slid down one of the escape roads, dropping from tenth to sixteenth, after his seat suddenly broke. 'I felt as though I was floating in the cockpit,' he later admitted. 'I made several mistakes due to this problem, as I often overshot the corners because I didn't have any feel in the brake pedal. In fact, sometimes I couldn't even reach the pedals.' Under the circumstances, Alex did well to avoid a major accident on this unyielding track.

BELOW Frank Williams in conversation with his drivers. All those who have driven for Williams' team quickly learn that Frank and Patrick Head have a pragmatic, down-to-earth approach to all their employees – and that includes the men behind the wheel. They are never mollycoddled or fussed over excessively, but if they give of their best, by the same token they are seldom given a hard time if they make the occasional mistake while pressing hard. Nevertheless, the 1999 season was a stressful one for Williams and his colleagues. The FW21 was not competitive and although Ralf Schumacher was growing progressively in stature in his new role, the three-year contract offered to Zanardi had quickly proved to be a major error and one that would be expensive when it came to negotiating a release from its balance at the end of the season.

ABOVE Golden moment for Ralf Schumacher in the rain-soaked French Grand Prix at Magny-Cours as his WilliamsF1 FW21 pulls level with big brother Michael's Ferrari in their tussle for fourth place. Ralf had been caught out by the changeable weather in qualifying and took a distant sixteenth on the grid, but in the race he stormed through the pack in great style to take fourth at the chequered flag ahead of his brother. Even so, he believed that a podium finish had been a distinct possibility. 'Our car was quicker today than our main competitors,' said Ralf, 'and we missed an opportunity.' Team-mate Alex Zanardi retired with an engine problem.

ABOVE Some you win, some you lose. Ralf Schumacher's generally impressive form during 1999 was blighted by a few disappointing mistakes. One such came early in the Austrian Grand Prix as he was trying to outbrake Pedro Diniz's Sauber C18 for fifth place and lost control, pirouetting to a halt with his rear wheels beached in a gravel trap. 'I braked too late and began to slide on the track, which was quite dirty at that point,' he freely conceded. 'I could not then avoid spinning and going into the gravel.' It was a bad day for WilliamsF1. Alex Zanardi missed three pit signals telling him to come in and ran out of fuel on the circuit as a result.

BELOW Ralf Schumacher shaves one of the high chicane kerbs on his way to a brilliant second place in the Italian Grand Prix behind Heinz-Harald Frentzen's Jordan. In the early stages of the race an on-form Alex Zanardi had held third place ahead of Ralf, but obligingly moved over after eighteen laps. 'He made it incredibly easy for me to get by him to drive my own race and deserves a big share of my second place today,' said Ralf generously. In the closing stages Schumacher really piled on the pressure and finished just under four seconds behind the winning Jordan while Zanardi faded to seventh, a disappointment after his best-ever fourth place on the starting grid.

BELOW Alex Zanardi was the first retirement in the Hungarian Grand Prix at Budapest when his WilliamsF1 FW21 suffered a differential malfunction. Both he and Ralf Schumacher had complained about lack of grip during qualifying in which they had only managed to set fifteenth- and sixteenth-fastest times, respectively. Ralf finished a lapped ninth at the end of one of the team's worst races of the season, the young German driver making the best of his climb through the field from his lowly grid position. By this stage in the season it was becoming clear that Zanardi had little future with the team, his failure to get to grips with the intricacies of the F1 business as baffling to the team as to himself.

Ralf Schumacher drove another terrific race to finish fourth in the European Grand Prix at the Nurburgring, although he might well have won had it not been for a slight misunderstanding over the radio to the WilliamsF1 pit. On lap forty-nine, as he took the lead, he radioed in to say he thought he had picked up a puncture in a rear tyre, but by the time he relayed the message he was level with the pit-lane entrance and was obliged to stay out for another lap. Two corners later the suspect rear tyre flew apart and he hobbled back to the pits on three wheels for a replacement to be fitted. That dropped him to fifth. He eventually made up a place before the end of the race, which was won by Johnny Herbert's Stewart-Ford.

LEFT Against an angry sky Alex Zanardi heads towards the end of what would prove to be the penultimate F1 outing of his career. After he had parked his WilliamsF1 FW21 for the last time there would follow months of behind-the-scenes negotiation before it was formally confirmed that he would not be seeing out the second and third seasons of his contract. In 2000 the charismatic Italian driver would enjoy a spell of semi-retirement but returned to the US-based CART series in 2001, driving for Morris Nunn's Indianapolis-based team. Tragically, he would be involved in a freak accident during the CART round at Germany's Lausitzring circuit in which he lost both legs below the knee. Within months, the popular Zanardi was already learning to walk again with artificial limbs, a testament to his zest for life and burning determination to enjoy it.

ABOVE BMW's partnership with WilliamsF1 took off seriously during 1999 on the international sports car scene when it constructed the bespoke V12-engined LMR endurance racer at a separate facility within its factory complex at Grove. Here Joachim Winkelhock is seen at the wheel of the LMR that would win Le Mans after a robust battle with its rivals Toyota on a weekend when the Mercedes CLRs suffered from such severe aerodynamic imbalances that they had to be withdrawn from the race.

LEFT The entrance to the impressive WilliamsF1 headquarters at Grove, near Wantage, in Oxfordshire, to which the company moved in 1996 after a nineteen-year split between two locations in Didcot. The new facility would permit sufficient potential for expansion, including the eventual incorporation of a separate building from which the BMW Le Mans project would be run, as well as extra office space for the commercial and marketing department that was fast expanding. WilliamsF1 has become such an important employer in the area that a roundabout was built on the main road outside the premises in order to ease the traffic flow during peak periods when the 400-strong workforce was arriving and departing.

RIGHT For the 2000 season the WilliamsF1 team gained a distinctive new blue and white livery to mark its new engine partnership with BMW – and the arrival of twenty-year-old Jenson Button as the team's replacement for Alex Zanardi. The selection of Button, an impressive Formula 3 performer during the previous season, came about after a great deal of detailed thought and analysis by the WilliamsF1 management. Button had briefly tested a Prost F1 car at Barcelona before Christmas and proved instantly impressive, a performance that alerted Frank Williams to his potential. In the end it came down to a shootout at Jerez between Jenson and the team's test driver, Bruno Junquiera, to determine which of them got the drive. Button's relaxed demeanour behind the wheel of a Grand Prix car, combined with his obvious and instinctive talent, won him the day.

LEFT The official launch of the WilliamsF1 BMW FW22 with Ralf Schumacher in the cockpit and test driver Bruno Junqueira alongside. The FW22 was a totally new car, designed to accommodate the 72-degree V10 type E41 BMW engine that had been developed totally in-house by the Munich-based car maker that had been out of the F1 business for more than a decade. The design of the new car was again the responsibility of technical teams directed by Gavin Fisher and Geoff Willis, with the principal initial challenge for the season being to achieve reliability from the new engine. 'The new car had some similarities to last year's FW21,' said Patrick Head. 'We worked to build on the strong points of that car, while eliminating its low points, particularly its poor aerodynamic performance on high-downforce circuits.'

RIGHT Frank Williams and Ralf Schumacher concentrate hard on the timing screens, while BMW competitions manager Gerhard Berger watches in familiar pose, his arms folded and an impassive expression on his face. Everybody on both sides of the BMW–WilliamsF1 partnership was impressed at how Gerhard took to his new role like a duck to water, confounding those sceptics who believed that the former F1 winner had too much of a free-wheeling personality to knuckle down to such a disciplined task. His commitment to the job in hand proved to be outstanding and he showed himself to be firm with the team management when fighting BMW's corner. Asked why he'd never driven for Williams during his F1 career, he used to joke, 'Frank would never offer enough money.'

TOP LEFT Ralf Schumacher's WilliamsF1 BMW FW22 refuelling in the first race of the season, the Australian Grand Prix at Melbourne. Ralf qualified eleventh for this event and opted to use the spare car for the race, but kept out of trouble and picked his way through to third at the finish behind the Ferraris of his elder brother Michael and Rubens Barrichello. It was quite an achievement at the end of the first outing for the BMW WilliamsF1 partnership. Jenson Button crashed in practice, qualified on the back row of the grid but hung on to the tail of the midfield bunch in bold and confident style before being sidelined with engine failure.

ABOVE LEFT Ralf Schumacher during pre-season testing at Barcelona's Circuit de Catalunya with the WilliamsF1 BMW FW22. Much of the BMW V10's early running had been carried out since September 1999 in an uprated FW21B development car, a task that included surmounting an early oil system problem that arose only when the engine was installed in the chassis and not when it was being tested on a dynamometer. The season would unfold in moderately promising style with the new BMW WilliamsF1 alliance ending up third in the Constructors' Championship behind Ferrari and McLaren. It was premature to say that WilliamsF1 was back to its dominant position, but it had certainly turned the corner.

Jenson Button in the WilliamsF1 BMW FW22 on his way to a fine sixth place behind team-mate Ralf Schumacher in the Brazilian Grand Prix, only his second F1 outing. For many laps during the race Button was locked in a wheel-to-wheel battle with Dutch driver Jos Verstappen's promising Arrows A21, eventually getting ahead of his rival in a decisive overtaking manoeuvre fifteen laps from the finish. Button drove with great maturity and self-control in what many observers regarded as one of the best performances in the race. It was early days for Jenson, of course, but already the signs were extremely promising.

Ralf Schumacher at speed in the San Marino
Grand Prix at Imola, the third round of the World
Championship which saw him run briefly in third
place before retiring with a fuel pick-up problem.
Jenson Button had dropped out with engine trouble
after only five laps, so this was a generally
disappointing early performance by the team.
'Unfortunately, I was delayed at the start, losing four
places and dropping to ninth,' said Ralf. 'After that
I gradually moved up to fifth and after Jacques
Villeneuve went in for his pit stop, I could push
a little harder. Unfortunately then I had my problems.'

RIGHT Red flags at Monaco bring the Grand Prix to a halt midway round the opening lap with Pedro de la Rosa's Arrows broadside across the circuit in front of Jenson Button's WilliamsF1 BMW at the Loews Hairpin. The Spanish driver had boldly attempted to run around the outside of Button at this corner, but Jenson had inadvertently tipped him into a spin. The two cars shuddered to a halt and there was nowhere else for any of the others to go. Button ran back to the pits where he took the spare WilliamsF1 FW22 for the restart, but he lasted only sixteen laps before retiring with fluctuating oil pressure. It was also a bad race for Ralf Schumacher, who crashed quite heavily at Ste Devote, suffering a badly cut left leg in the impact.

LEFT Portent for the future. Jorg Muller in the Michelin-liveried WilliamsF1 FW21B test car evaluating the French company's F1 rubber in preparation for Michelin's return to the Grand Prix scene at the start of 2001. WilliamsF1 decided that there was more chance of getting a performance boost in the battle against Ferrari by switching from Bridgestone tyres. Michelin had last competed in F1 back in 1984 when they were used to great advantage by the McLaren team which won twelve out of the season's sixteen races with the French company. Within the WilliamsF1 BMW camp there was huge optimism about changing to Michelin for the following year.

RIGHT Ralf Schumacher's WilliamsF1 BMW FW22 being manoeuvred by team mechanics in the pit lane at Spa-Francorchamps during the Belgian Grand Prix weekend. With Ralf qualifying sixth, three places behind Jenson Button, who was also ahead of Michael Schumacher, it promised to be a good race for the team, but the Englishman unfortunately became embroiled in an early collision with Jarno Trulli and dropped back to fifth at the end of a race that he felt should have delivered him considerably more. Ralf kept out of trouble and had a relatively lonely race to third place, but it was heartening that the FW22s had run reliably on this occasion and both scored points. Jenson later reflected, 'I thought I could only out-qualify Michael Schumacher if he had fallen off the track or something.'

Jenson Button swings his WilliamsF1 BMW FW22 into the pit chicane at Suzuka ahead of Johnny Herbert's Jaguar, Jacques Villeneuve's BAR-Honda and Jos Verstappen's Arrows during the early stages of the Japanese Grand Prix. He qualified fifth for this race, one place ahead of Ralf Schumacher, and drove a good race to take two points. 'My start was quite disastrous,' he confessed. 'Having started fifth, I dropped back to seventh, but kept pushing as hard as I could. The car was well balanced and working very well, which enabled me to put in quite good lap times, although obviously not as good as Ferrari and McLaren ahead of me.'

LEFT F1 technology at its cutting edge. A scale model in the WilliamsF1 wind tunnel, one of the key weapons in any F1 team's armoury for the past decade or more. Aerodynamic development in today's highly complex motor-racing business involves huge investment to obtain minuscule gains in car performance. Wind tunnels have gradually become more sophisticated over the past few years and the challenge of building one is more than matched by the intricate business of calibrating it correctly so that the results obtained translate accurately to performance improvements on the completed car. By the end of the 2002 season WilliamsF1 was busy finalising the concept of an even more sophisticated wind-tunnel facility that it hopes to have operational at Grove in 2004.

RIGHT A delighted Ralf Schumacher waves to the crowd as he cruises during his slowing-down lap after winning the San Marino Grand Prix at Imola, his first F1 victory and the maiden success for the BMW WilliamsF1 partnership. The German driver led for every one of the race's sixty-two laps and brought to an end a run of fifty-four races without a victory for the WilliamsF1 team. It was also the first win for Michelin since their F1 return at the start of the season and established the Schumacher brothers as the only siblings ever to have won Grands Prix in the fifty-two-season history of the official World Championship. More importantly, Ralf's success signalled that there was now a third force on the contemporary F1 scene.

LEFT The new WilliamsF1 FW23 was propelled by a brand-new, state-of-the-art 90-degree BMW type P80 V10 from the start of the season, and it became immediately clear that this combination had the potential to get on terms with the pace-setting Ferrari and McLaren opposition. Here Juan Pablo Montoya, who replaced Jenson Button at the start of the season as Ralf Schumacher's team-mate, powers ahead of Michael Schumacher's Ferrari during the Brazilian Grand Prix after a bold overtaking manoeuvre going into the first corner. He was pulling away from the field when he was rammed off the road by Jos Verstappen's Arrows, which he had just lapped at the end of the long back straight. It was a huge disappointment for Montoya, but he was at least satisfied to have laid down a marker for the future in what was only his third F1 race outing.

Ralf Schumacher's WilliamsF1 BMW FW22 swoops over a rise at the spectacular A1-Ring circuit during the 2000 Austrian Grand Prix, an event that proved extremely frustrating for both the German driver and his British team-mate Jenson Button. During qualifying both men struggled with acute lack of adhesion on the track's notoriously low-grip surface, ending a distant eighteenth and nineteenth on the starting grid. Button finished fifth, but Ralf was eventually forced to retire after a succession of brake problems dropped him out of contention early on. It was all very frustrating for the team in the first season of its new partnership with BMW.

LEFT Ralf Schumacher on the winner's rostrum at Imola after his first Grand Prix victory, celebrating the very special day that his brother Michael had first experienced a decade earlier when he won the 1992 Belgian Grand Prix. Ralf later recalled, 'I remember the moment I was told that Frank Williams was interested in me being one of his two drivers for the Williams team as if it were only a few days ago. It is one of the warmest memories I have in Formula One: me, Ralf Schumacher, driving for Williams – incredible! Driving for a team with such an immense motorsport tradition, driving for a man like Frank Williams. For me as a young driver he was like a godfather of motorsport: warm, with a special sense of humour which I love, straight in his mind. The success of his team is reflected in his character and vice versa. And then I climbed the podium for my first victory in Formula One and for the WilliamsF1 team and I wasn't only happy for myself; I was proud to be able to give something back to the team. I was proud to be a part of this team.'

RIGHT The entire WilliamsF1 BMW crew celebrating Ralf's victory at Imola. This shot gives an idea of the scale of the investment in personnel by every major F1 team. On this occasion it was also good to see that key Michelin personnel – on the right, in blue and yellow shirts – had been invited to share the occasion. The high-tech motorhomes in the background were new for the 2001 season, reflecting the effort that goes into keeping the team's principal investors happy when they visit a race, as well as providing a tranquil base from where the engineers and senior management can operate. It was certainly a far cry from where Frank WilliamsF1 started in F1, changing gear ratios on Piers Courage's Brabham in gravel-strewn paddocks more than thirty years earlier.

LEFT Juan Pablo Montoya's WilliamsF1 FW23 stands on the grid at Barcelona's Circuit de Catalunya prior to the start of the Spanish Grand Prix, the race in which the Colombian driver would score his first podium finish with a second place behind Michael Schumacher's victorious Ferrari. On a day when Ralf Schumacher threw away a possible fourth-place finish with a spin into a gravel trap, Montoya saved the day for the team with a strong showing. This was the race at which the technical regulations permitted the readmission of anti-wheelspin traction-control systems, but the team did not use theirs because they felt it needed further development before it was perfect. After this fifth round of the World Championship WilliamsF1 held third place in the Constructors' Championship table with Ralf Schumacher fourth in the drivers' rankings.

RIGHT Ralf Schumacher leads Juan Pablo Montoya during the Monaco Grand Prix, in which both WilliamsF1 BMWs retired from the fray. Montoya got a little carried away by the enormity of the occasion, set the fastest lap and then glanced the wall going into the S-bend at the swimming pool with his left rear wheel. He crashed out of the race at the next corner and freely conceded that it had been all his fault. For much of the race Ralf held third place but eventually came into the pits after fifty-eight laps with what were diagnosed as hydraulic problems. 'A warning light came on,' he explained, 'then the power steering failed and finally as I came into the pits the gear-change packed up and the engine cut out.'

Ralf Schumacher carved another slice of F1 history in the Canadian
Grand Prix at Montreal when his WilliamsF1 BMW headed
brother Michael's Ferrari past the chequered flag. It ensured that
the German brothers were the first siblings to finish first and second
in a World Championship Grand Prix. It may have been against the
historical odds for Ralf to be the one who came out on top on this
unique occasion, but by making his crucial single refuelling stop
later than Michael he emerged ahead for the closing sprint to the
line and was never again challenged. As Mika Hakkinen, who
finished third, jocularly remarked after the podium ceremony,
'Thank God there aren't three of them.'

The European Grand Prix at the Nurburgring inevitably attracted a capacity crowd to witness the latest contest
between the Schumacher brothers. Michael's Ferrari just pipped Ralf's WilliamsF1 BMW to pole position
on the grid for the sixty-seven-lap race. On this occasion it was Michael who raced to a hard-fought and ultimately
commanding victory after his wheel-to-wheel battle with Ralf was defused unexpectedly. As the WilliamsF1 driver
emerged from his first refuelling stop, he mistakenly ran over the white line delineating the track proper from the
pit exit lane. It was an infringement that earned him a ten-second stop–go penalty that dropped him back to fourth
place at the chequered flag and permitted Juan Pablo Montoya to finish second in the other FW23.

Mobil 1 Mobil 1 Mobil 1 Mobil 1 Mobil 1 Mobil 1 Mobil 1 Mobil 1
Mobil 1
Mobil 1 Mobil 1

LEFT The huge stadium complex at Hockenheim provides a stirring sight for race fans at the start of the German Grand Prix, with Juan Pablo Montoya accelerating his WilliamsF1 BMW FW23 into an immediate lead from pole position ahead of team-mate Ralf Schumacher's sister car. Behind are the McLarens of Mika Hakkinen and David Coulthard and the two Ferraris of Michael Schumacher and Rubens Barrichello. Juan Pablo built up a decisive advantage only to succumb to engine failure, allowing Ralf to take his third victory of the season thus far. It was another historic success for the BMW WilliamsF1 team, as not since the legendary Rudolf Caracciola took the 1939 German Grand Prix in a Mercedes had the race been won by a German driver powered by a German engine. It was quite a cause for celebration, even though it had definitely been an unlucky event for the hapless Montoya.

ABOVE Montoya's WilliamsF1 BMW leads the chase of Michael Schumacher's leading Ferrari in the opening stages of the US Grand Prix at Indianapolis, with Rubens Barrichello's Ferrari, Ralf Schumacher and the McLarens of Mika Hakkinen and David Coulthard hanging on close behind. Montoya raced Schumacher energetically, but his hopes of winning in F1 at this same venue where he had been victorious in the Indy 500 just eighteen months earlier were thwarted by a hydraulic failure after thirty-eight laps. 'It was a bit disappointing as I think we could have got a win here – which would have been my second – and back-to-back wins would have been brilliant,' he reflected. Ralf spun off a lap before Montoya retired, frankly admitting that he'd made a mistake and couldn't blame the error on anybody but himself.

profile

Juan Pablo Montoya

'There is no secret to this business,' insists Juan Pablo Montoya. 'You work to improve your car, then it goes round corners better and then you are faster. Everybody thinks that Michael wins because there is some Schumacher magic. The guy is bloody good, but he has a terrific team behind him. He's not doing anything different to anybody else. He's just driving the car and the car is quicker. Simple.'

Montoya is unabashed by his perceived status as the man most likely to topple the elder Schumacher brother from his position at the pinnacle of Formula One. 'Yeah, I think a lot of people think that,' he says. 'But, to be honest, I don't think about it and don't care about it. I am just doing my thing with my engineers and the mechanics and hope it will produce a good result each weekend.'

This straightforward thinking characterises the popular Colombian driver who first joined the Williams line-up at the start of the 2001 season and won his first Grand Prix at Monza later that year.

'Williams means a lot to me,' he says. 'Great people, great team: it's largely thanks to Frank that I'm here. I first met him at Silverstone in 1997 when Jacques Villeneuve won the team its one hundredth Grand Prix victory. I was doing Formula 3000. In 1998 I was invited to test for the team and continued to do Formula 3000 before I went to America. I really enjoyed that 1998 season testing for Williams and I think I learned a lot. I was looking forward to trying to get the race seat for 1999 and was very disappointed when I didn't eventually get the drive, because I was regularly on the pace with the two team drivers.

'I get on really well with Frank. I think he has done great things for the sport and great things with his team over the years – and he clearly wants to do so again. Patrick is Patrick, of course. A really nice guy who knows a lot about the business, but can be quite explosive. He gets very excited about things – and it can sometimes be difficult

when he's like that – but he's obviously a huge asset for the team and great fun to work for.

'We're determined to dominate again. Ferrari may be kicking everybody's ass for the moment, but I truly believe that Williams has a very bright future. Everybody in the team wants to resume those winning ways and you sense that everybody at the track and at the factory is working very hard to get there. I hope I can be part of that. There is a great sense of community at Williams. You feel at home here. I don't feel above anybody, just one part of the team. It's a great feeling and everybody has pride in the team.'

OPPOSITE Juan Pablo Montoya dropped 3.8 seconds behind Michael Schumacher's leading Ferrari on the opening lap of the Japanese Grand Prix and it was half a dozen laps before his Michelin tyres worked up to their optimum performance levels. Schumacher maintained his advantage for the remainder of the race, but Montoya kept pressing all the way to the chequered flag to round off his maiden F1 season with another strong second place. He even escaped without penalty after straight-lining the pit chicane on one occasion. Ralf Schumacher did it twice and collected a ten-second stop–go penalty as a result, which dropped him back to sixth at the end of the race. With four wins to their credit the BMW WilliamsF1 team finished the year third in the Constructors' Championship just twenty-two points behind McLaren. However, their tally was less than half that posted by the dominant Ferraris.

ABOVE A spectacular shot of Juan Pablo Montoya's winning Williams BMW catapulting out of Parabolica to cross the start/finish line at Monza with the Alpine peaks in the distance. Montoya raced closely with Rubens Barrichello's Ferrari for much of the way and emerged victorious after a drive that reflected a great balance of aggression and restraint from start to finish. It was the fourth BMW WilliamsF1 victory of the season and one that saw Ralf Schumacher – who'd scored the other three – trailing home a slightly disappointed third. The whole weekend took place in a slightly subdued atmosphere following the terrorist outrages in New York earlier in the week, and both Schumacher brothers had seemed particularly affected.

Visitors to the WilliamsF1 Conference Centre and Grand Prix Collection at Grove will find a representative selection of the team's Formula One cars from the past twenty-five seasons, including (TOP LEFT) this impressive line-up of its Renault-engined contenders. The Williams-Renault FW19 driven by Jacques Villeneuve during 1997 forms one of the elaborately suspended centrepiece attractions at the WilliamsF1 Conference Centre and Grand Prix Collection (TOP RIGHT), in which the cars on show are displayed in imaginative and striking settings. The conference centre has been a great success. Hundreds of race fans regularly turn up to watch televised Grand Prix coverage from the comfort of its theatre while enjoying the added benefit of direct briefings from the various circuits by key team members. With a champagne breakfast and lunch as part of the day's package, it represents a great day out for WilliamsF1 supporters. The achievements of former Williams World Champions Alan Jones and Keke Rosberg are highlighted in this dramatic display (BOTTOM RIGHT). In the background are Williams

FW07s, as driven by Jones between 1979 and 1981, while in the centre of the picture is the FW08 that Rosberg drove to become World Champion in 1982. Closest to the camera is the six-wheeler version of the FW08 tested by Rosberg during 1982 before a change in the F1 regulations banned its use the following year.

BOTTOM LEFT Every bit as impressive as the exhibition of WilliamsF1 cars is the magnificent display of trophies accumulated by so many of the team's great drivers over the past three decades. All these are on show in subtly illuminated glass-fronted cabinets in the WilliamsF1 Conference Centre and Grand Prix Collection as a testament to the team's achievements. The sheer diversity of shapes and styles is certainly arresting, although the taste displayed by some race organisers in their trophies is eclectic, to say the least. Both drivers' and teams' performances attract the award of silverware, but while the first three drivers receive a trophy, only a race win earns the team an addition to its trophy cabinet.

RIGHT It may have been wet [ ] damp and cold at Silverstone [ ] the launch of the new WilliamsF1 BMW FW24, b[ ] Juan Pablo Montoya injected [ ] some welcome warmth into t[ ] proceedings by enthusing ove[ ] the performance of the new P[ ] BMW V10 engine. Williams[ ] chief designer Gavin Fisher described the FW24 as an evolutionary version of last ye[ ] car, emphasising that there we[ ] no major technical rule chang[ ] for the 2002 season. Yet the design team at WilliamsF1 ha[ ] to develop and install a completely new engine, which[ ] turn required the developmen[ ] of a totally new gearbox and associated changes to the remainder of the drive train. BMW Motorsport director Mario Theissen made the poi[ ] that in addition to more powe[ ] and enhanced reliability, the BMW design team had worke[ ] hard to reduce the weight at t[ ] top of the new P82 V10 engir[ ] in the interests of optimising t[ ] car's centre of gravity. Twenty [ ] cent of the engine has been changed to achieve this. All th[ ] core components – such as the[ ] cylinder head, crankcase, crankshaft, camshaft and electronic management system[ ] – are developed and manufactured at BMW in Munich.

Ralf Schumacher showers the champagne to celebrate his well-judged victory in the 2002 Malaysian Grand Prix ahead of his team-mate Juan Pablo Montoya, the first WilliamsF1 one–two finish since Jacques Villeneuve and Damon Hill in the Portuguese Grand Prix almost six years earlier. 'The team did a fantastic job,' enthused Schumacher. 'The car was just there, almost perfect for the whole race, especially the second stint where there was even more rubber on the circuit. It was just an easy game. I still can't believe it, to be honest. It's all down to the team, I must say.' Montoya, who had survived a first-corner collision with Michael Schumacher's Ferrari and then a 'drive-through' penalty as a result, echoed his team-mate's contentment with the car. 'After the start, I thought my race was over,' he said with a grin. 'I thought that I will try to push and try to get one or two points, and here I am with six. It's pretty good.'

Juan Pablo Montoya leads Ralf Schumacher at Monza during practice for the 2002 Italian Grand Prix. However, this scenario was not repeated in the race for more than a few hundred yards. Accelerating away from the starting grid, Ralf barged through to take the lead from the second row, but then straight-lined the first corner, which clearly put him in the firing line for a possible penalty from the stewards. Fortuitously, all the teams on the pit wall are now connected with the officials in race control via email, so the crew was able to check that there would be no penalty applied if Ralf conceded the lead to Montoya. Back came the OK and the signal went out to the German driver. Accordingly, Ralf eased back as he came out of Parabolica at the end of the fourth lap. As Juan Pablo surged past, Ralf's BMW engine expired, leaving the Colombian to battle alone against the Ferraris.

The 2002 Italian Grand Prix was a race at which hopes were running high that Juan Pablo Montoya might repeat his maiden F1 victory of twelve months earlier. Sure enough, he scythed a path to pole position at an average speed of 161.170 m.p.h. This beat the previous F1 closed-circuit record of 160.397 m.p.h. that had been established by Keke Rosberg's Williams-Honda FW10 turbo while qualifying for pole position at the 1985 British Grand Prix at Silverstone. Unfortunately, the race proved less of a success for Montoya. While initially he mixed it with the Ferraris, he damaged his WilliamsF1 FW24 with a trip across one of the chicane run-off areas and fell back into a distant third place. Eventually he retired from the race with a suspension problem.

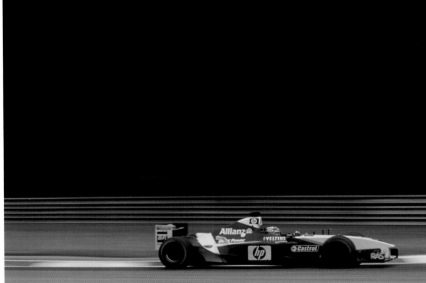

LEFT The final moments on the grid before the start of a Grand Prix are both tense and exacting. Here the WilliamsF1 crew moves with unobtrusive efficiency around Juan Pablo Montoya's car in the moments prior to the start of the 2002 United States Grand Prix at Indianapolis. Tyre warmers are in place, the car fuelled up and ready to go, but experienced eyes are still checking every detail to ensure that no last-moment snags should occur. In a few moments Montoya will be strapped into the cockpit, he will check the adjustment of his rear-view mirrors, the car's BMW engine will be fired up and he will accelerate away on the pre-race formation lap.

RIGHT Juan Pablo Montoya's WilliamsF1 BMW FW24 against the scenic backdrop at Indianapolis during the 2002 United States Grand Prix. This was a rather unfortunate outing for the BMW-WilliamsF1 team .When Montoya went to overtake Ralf Schumacher going into the first corner after the pits at the end of the opening lap the German driver inadvertently rode up the inside kerb and spun into the other Williams, knocking them both off the track and removing his own rear wing. A furious Montoya recovered quickly but dropped to seventh, while Schumacher drove slowly round to the pits for a replacement wing before resuming in a distant last place. Later, Montoya made a tactical error when he misunderstood instructions from his pit and came in to refuel about nine laps earlier than expected. He eventually finished fourth, close behind David Coulthard's McLaren, while Ralf ended right down the field, albeit running strongly to the finish after that initial slip.

Ancient and modern.
Ralf Schumacher's
WilliamsF1 BMW FW24
accelerates down the pit
lane at Indianapolis during
the 2002 United States
Grand Prix, crossing the
strip of brick that stands
as a memorial to the early
days of the famous
American track when it
was entirely surfaced in
this manner, thereby
producing its familiar
nickname 'The Brickyard'.

This striking shot shows Juan Pablo Montoya's WilliamsF1 BMW FW24 heading for fourth place in the 2002 Japanese Grand Prix at Suzuka, a race during which he was initially frustrated by a handling imbalance that was partially cured by a quick adjustment of the front-wing settings during a routine refuelling stop. During Friday's free practice session Montoya crashed quite heavily at the tricky right-hand Degner Curve. 'I went on to the throttle like always and thought I was going to make the corner fine,' said the shaken Colombian driver, 'but instead I went over the sharp part of the kerb and lost the car. The impact was hard and I am still a bit sore.'

108 Grand Prix Victories (as at end of 2002 season)

FIA Formula One World Constructors' Champions

1980
1981
1986
1987
1992
1993
1994
1996
1997

Year	Date	Grand Prix	Circuit	Driver
1979	14.07.	Britain	Silverstone	Clay Regazzoni
	29.07.	Germany	Hockenheim	Alan Jones
	12.08.	Austria	Österreichring	Alan Jones
	26.08.	Holland	Zandvoort	Alan Jones
	30.09.	Canada	Montreal	Alan Jones
1980	13.01.	Argentina	Buenos Aires	Alan Jones
	18.05.	Monaco	Monte Carlo	Carlos Reutemann
	29.06.	France	Le Castellet	Alan Jones
	13.07.	Britain	Brands Hatch	Alan Jones
	28.09.	Canada	Montreal	Alan Jones
	05.10.	USA East	Watkins Glen	Alan Jones
1981	15.03.	USA West	Long Beach	Alan Jones
	29.03.	Brazil	Jacarepagua	Carlos Reutemann
	17.05.	Belgium	Zolder	Carlos Reutemann
	17.10.	USA	Las Vegas	Alan Jones
1982	29.08.	Switzerland	Dijon	Keke Rosberg
1983	15.05.	Monaco	Monte Carlo	Keke Rosberg
1984	08.07.	USA	Dallas	Keke Rosberg
1985	23.06.	USA	East Detroit	Keke Rosberg
	06.10.	Europe	Brands Hatch	Nigel Mansell
	19.10.	South Africa	Kyalami	Nigel Mansell
	03.11.	Australia	Adelaide	Keke Rosberg
1986	23.03.	Brazil	Jacarepagua	Nelson Piquet
	25.05.	Belgium	Spa	Nigel Mansell
	15.06.	Canada	Montreal	Nigel Mansell
	06.07.	France	Le Castellet	Nigel Mansell
	13.07.	Britain	Brands Hatch	Nigel Mansell
	27.07.	Germany	Hockenheim	Nelson Piquet
	10.08.	Hungary	Hungaroring	Nelson Piquet
	17.08.	Italy	Monza	Nelson Piquet
	21.09.	Portugal	Estoril	Nigel Mansell
1987	13.05.	San Marino	Imola	Nigel Mansell
	05.07.	France	Le Castellet	Nigel Mansell
	12.07.	Britain	Silverstone	Nigel Mansell
	26.07.	Germany	Hockenheim	Nelson Piquet
	09.08.	Hungary	Hungaroring	Nelson Piquet
	16.08.	Austria	Österreichring	Nigel Mansell
	06.09.	Italy	Monza	Nelson Piquet
	27.09.	Spain	Jerez	Nigel Mansell
	18.10.	Mexico	Mexico City	Nigel Mansell
1989	18.06.	Canada	Montreal	Thierry Boutsen
	05.11.	Australia	Adelaide	Thierry Boutsen
1990	13.05.	San Marino	Imola	Riccardo Patrese
	12.08.	Hungary	Hungaroring	Thierry Boutsen
1991	16.06.	Mexico	Mexico City	Riccardo Patrese
	07.07.	France	Magny-Cours	Nigel Mansell
	14.07.	Britain	Silverstone	Nigel Mansell
	28.07.	Germany	Hockenheim	Nigel Mansell
	08.09.	Italy	Monza	Nigel Mansell
	22.09.	Portugal	Estoril	Riccardo Patrese
	29.09.	Spain	Barcelona	Nigel Mansell
1992	01.03.	South Africa	Kyalami	Nigel Mansell
	22.03.	Mexico	Mexico City	Nigel Mansell
	05.04.	Brazil	Interlagos	Nigel Mansell
	03.05.	Spain	Barcelona	Nigel Mansell
	17.05.	San Marino	Imola	Nigel Mansell
	05.07.	France	Magny-Cours	Nigel Mansell
	12.07.	Britain	Silverstone	Nigel Mansell
	26.07.	Germany	Hockenheim	Nigel Mansell
	27.09.	Portugal	Estoril	Nigel Mansell
	25.10.	Japan	Suzuka	Riccardo Patrese
1993	14.03.	South Africa	Kyalami	Alain Prost
	25.04.	San Marino	Imola	Alain Prost
	09.05.	Spain	Barcelona	Alain Prost
	13.06.	Canada	Montreal	Alain Prost
	04.07.	France	Magny-Cours	Alain Prost
	11.07.	Britain	Silverstone	Alain Prost
	25.07.	Germany	Hockenheim	Alain Prost
	15.08.	Hungary	Hungaroring	Damon Hill
	29.08.	Belgium	Spa	Damon Hill
	12.09.	Italy	Monza	Damon Hill
1994	29.05.	Spain	Barcelona	Damon Hill
	10.07.	Britain	Silverstone	Damon Hill
	28.08.	Belgium	Spa	Damon Hill
	11.09.	Italy	Monza	Damon Hill
	25.09.	Portugal	Estoril	Damon Hill
	06.11.	Japan	Suzuka	Damon Hill
	14.11.	Australia	Adelaide	Nigel Mansell
1995	09.04.	Argentina	Buenos Aires	Damon Hill
	30.04.	San Marino	Imola	Damon Hill
	13.08.	Hungary	Hungaroring	Damon Hill
	24.09.	Portugal	Estoril	David Coulthard
	12.11.	Australia	Adelaide	Damon Hill
1996	10.03.	Australia	Melbourne	Damon Hill
	31.03.	Brazil	Interlagos	Damon Hill
	07.04.	Argentina	Buenos Aires	Damon Hill
	28.04.	Europe	Nürburgring	Jacques Villeneuve
	05.05.	San Marino	Imola	Damon Hill
	16.06.	Canada	Montreal	Damon Hill
	30.06.	France	Magny-Cours	Damon Hill
	14.07.	Britain	Silverstone	Jacques Villeneuve
	28.07.	Germany	Hockenheim	Damon Hill
	11.08.	Hungary	Hungaroring	Jacques Villeneuve
	22.09.	Portugal	Estoril	Jacques Villeneuve
	13.10.	Japan	Suzuka	Damon Hill
1997	30.03.	Brazil	Interlagos	Jacques Villeneuve
	13.04.	Argentina	Buenos Aires	Jacques Villeneuve
	27.04.	San Marino	Imola	Heinz-Harald Frentzen
	25.05.	Spain	Barcelona	Jacques Villeneuve
	13.07.	Britain	Silverstone	Jacques Villeneuve
	10.08.	Hungary	Hungaroring	Jacques Villeneuve
	21.09.	Austria	A1 Ring	Jacques Villeneuve
	28.09.	Luxembourg	Nürburgring	Jacques Villeneuve
2001	15.04.	San Marino	Imola	Ralf Schumacher
	10.06.	Canada	Montreal	Ralf Schumacher
	29.07.	Germany	Hockenheim	Ralf Schumacher
	16.09.	Italy	Monza	Juan Pablo Montoya
2002	17.03	Malaysia	Sepang	Ralf Schumacher

WILLIAMSF1: Twenty-Five years at a Glance

119 Pole Positions (as at end of 2001 season)

Year	Date	Grand Prix	Circuit	Driver
1979	14.07.	Britain	Silverstone	Alan Jones
	30.09.	Canada	Montreal	Alan Jones
	07.10.	USA East	Watkins Glen	Alan Jones
1980	13.01.	Argentina	Buenos Aires	Alan Jones
	04.05.	Belgium	Zolder	Alan Jones
	10.08.	Germany	Hockenheim	Alan Jones
1981	17.05.	Belgium	Zolder	Carlos Reutemann
	17.10.	USA	Las Vegas	Carlos Reutemann
1982	18.07.	Britain	Brands Hatch	Keke Rosberg
1983	13.03.	Brazil	Jacarepagua	Keke Rosberg
1985	07.07.	France	Le Castellet	Keke Rosberg
	21.07.	Britain	Silverstone	Keke Rosberg
	19.10.	South Africa	Kyalami	Nigel Mansell
1986	25.05.	Belgium	Spa	Nelson Piquet
	15.06.	Canada	Montreal	Nigel Mansell
	13.07.	Britain	Brands Hatch	Nelson Piquet
	26.10.	Australia	Adelaide	Nigel Mansell
1987	12.04.	Brazil	Jacarepagua	Nigel Mansell
	17.05.	Belgium	Spa	Nigel Mansell
	31.05.	Monaco	Monte Carlo	Nigel Mansell
	21.06.	USA East	Detroit	Nigel Mansell
	05.07.	France	Le Castellet	Nigel Mansell
	12.07.	Britain	Silverstone	Nelson Piquet
	26.07.	Germany	Hockenheim	Nigel Mansell
	09.08.	Hungary	Hungaroring	Nigel Mansell
	16.08.	Austria	Österreichring	Nelson Piquet
	06.09.	Italy	Monza	Nelson Piquet
	27.09.	Spain	Jerez	Nelson Piquet
	18.10.	Mexico	Mexico City	Nigel Mansell
1989	13.08.	Hungary	Hungaroring	Riccardo Patrese
1990	12.08.	Hungary	Hungaroring	Thierry Boutsen
1991	02.06.	Canada	Montreal	Riccardo Patrese
	16.06.	Mexico	Mexico City	Riccardo Patrese
	07.07.	France	Magny-Cours	Riccardo Patrese
	14.07.	Britain	Silverstone	Nigel Mansell
	28.07.	Germany	Hockenheim	Nigel Mansell
	22.09.	Portugal	Estoril	Riccardo Patrese
1992	01.03.	South Africa	Kyalami	Nigel Mansell
	22.03.	Mexico	Mexico City	Nigel Mansell
	05.04.	Brazil	Interlagos	Nigel Mansell
	03.05.	Spain	Barcelona	Nigel Mansell
	17.05.	San Marino	Imola	Nigel Mansell
	31.05.	Monaco	Monte Carlo	Nigel Mansell
	05.07.	France	Magny-Cours	Nigel Mansell
	12.07.	Britain	Silverstone	Nigel Mansell
	26.07.	Germany	Hockenheim	Nigel Mansell
	16.08.	Hungary	Hungaroring	Riccardo Patrese
	30.08.	Belgium	Spa	Nigel Mansell
	13.09.	Italy	Monza	Nigel Mansell
	27.09.	Portugal	Estoril	Nigel Mansell
	25.10.	Japan	Suzuka	Nigel Mansell
	08.11.	Australia	Adelaide	Nigel Mansell
1993	14.03.	South Africa	Kyalami	Alain Prost
	28.03.	Brazil	Interlagos	Alain Prost
	11.04.	Europe	Donington	Alain Prost
	25.04.	San Marino	Imola	Alain Prost
	09.05.	Spain	Barcelona	Alain Prost
	23.05.	Monaco	Monte Carlo	Alain Prost
	13.06.	Canada	Montreal	Alain Prost
	04.07.	France	Magny-Cours	Damon Hill
	11.07.	Britain	Silverstone	Alain Prost
	25.07.	Germany	Hockenheim	Alain Prost
	15.08.	Hungary	Hungaroring	Alain Prost
	29.08.	Belgium	Spa	Alain Prost
	12.09.	Italy	Monza	Alain Prost
	26.09.	Portugal	Estoril	Damon Hill
	24.10.	Japan	Suzuka	Alain Prost
1994	27.03.	Brazil	Interlagos	Ayrton Senna
	17.04.	Pacific	Aida	Ayrton Senna
	01.05.	San Marino	Imola	Ayrton Senna
	03.07.	France	Magny-Cours	Damon Hill
	10.07.	Britain	Silverstone	Damon Hill
	14.11.	Australia	Adelaide	Nigel Mansell
1995	26.03.	Brazil	Interlagos	Damon Hill
	09.04.	Argentina	Buenos Aires	David Coulthard
	28.05.	Monaco	Monte Carlo	Damon Hill
	02.07.	France	Magny-Cours	Damon Hill
	16.07.	Britain	Silverstone	Damon Hill
	30.07.	Germany	Hockenheim	Damon Hill
	13.08.	Hungary	Hungaroring	Damon Hill
	10.09.	Italy	Monza	David Coulthard
	24.09.	Portugal	Estoril	David Coulthard
	01.10.	Europe	Nürburgring	David Coulthard
	22.10.	Pacific	Aida	David Coulthard
	12.11.	Australia	Adelaide	Damon Hill
1996	10.03.	Australia	Melbourne	Jacques Villeneuve
	31.03.	Brazil	Interlagos	Damon Hill
	07.04.	Argentina	Buenos Aires	Damon Hill
	28.04.	Europe	Nürburgring	Damon Hill
	02.06.	Spain	Barcelona	Damon Hill
	16.06.	Canada	Montreal	Damon Hill
	14.07.	Britain	Silverstone	Damon Hill
	28.07.	Germany	Hockenheim	Damon Hill
	25.08.	Belgium	Spa	Jacques Villeneuve
	08.09.	Italy	Monza	Damon Hill
	22.09.	Portugal	Estoril	Damon Hill
	13.10.	Japan	Suzuka	Jacques Villeneuve
1997	09.03.	Australia	Melbourne	Jacques Villeneuve
	30.03.	Brazil	Interlagos	Jacques Villeneuve
	13.04.	Argentina	Buenos Aires	Jacques Villeneuve
	27.04.	San Marino	Imola	Jacques Villeneuve
	11.05.	Monaco	Monte Carlo	Heinz-Harald Frentzen
	25.05.	Spain	Barcelona	Jacques Villeneuve
	13.07.	Britain	Silverstone	Jacques Villeneuve
	24.08.	Belgium	Spa	Jacques Villeneuve
	21.09.	Austria	A1 Ring	Jacques Villeneuve
	12.10.	Japan	Suzuka	Jacques Villeneuve
	26.10.	Europe	Jerez	Jacques Villeneuve
2001	01.07.	France	Magny-Cours	Ralf Schumacher
	28.07.	Germany	Hockenheim	Juan Pablo Montoya
	01.09.	Belgium	Spa	Juan Pablo Montoya
	15.09.	Italy	Monza	Juan Pablo Montoya
2002	30.03.	Brazil	Interlagos	Juan Pablo Montoya
	25.04.	Monaco	Monte Carlo	Juan Pablo Montoya
	08.06.	Canada	Montreal	Juan Pablo Montoya
	22.06.	Europe	Nurburgring	Juan Pablo Montoya
	07.07.	Britain	Silverstone	Juan Pablo Montoya
	20.07.	France	Magny Cours	Juan Pablo Montoya
	14.09.	Italy	Monza	Juan Pablo Montoya

FIA Formula One World Drivers' Champions

1980	Alan Jones
1982	Keke Rosberg
1987	Nelson Piquet
1992	Nigel Mansell
1993	Alain Prost
1996	Damon Hill
1997	Jacques Villeneuve

First published in Great Britain in 2003 by Orion
an imprint of Orion Books Ltd
Orion House, 5 Upper St Martin's Lane, London WC2H 9EA

A CIP catalogue record for this book is available
from the British Library

ISBN 0 75285 606 5

Photographs supplied by Sutton Motorsport Images
Designed by Harry Green
Printed and bound by Printer Trento S.r.l.